A Garden Of Love

My instructions were to wait, so I stayed planted in my uncomfortable chair and listened to that horrid clock tick. Minutes were like eternity on a normal day, and on this one I waited for one hundred twenty of them. With a loud scrape, the front door of the office waiting room finally opened. Instead of a new patient, it was my mother, motioning for me to leave. She had obviously left by the rear door after Aunt Edie's exam and walked back around to the entrance to retrieve me. The sacredness of the rear exit was maintained. Only I was the infidel by walking out of the waiting room through the entrance door. I'm not sure it had ever been done before, and under any other circumstances it could have been the highlight of my young life.

Aunt Edie was waiting in the car, her face ashen and drawn. Not a word was spoken when my mother and I crossed the fifty feet to the curb. I knew better than to utter a sound. After the car moved into traffic and we were on our way toward home, my mother reached over and patted her sister's hand.

"Edith, Doctor Fleckner is the best surgeon in the city. He's going to help you. Besides, he may say it's nothing." Her voice sounded hopeful.

"Doc Hacook is never wrong." Aunt Edie's voice was a whisper, so I leaned forward to hear better. My mother's backwards look flashed a warning and I sat back in my seat. "I'm going to die."

"No you are not," my mother flashed angrily. "You are absolutely not going to die and I don't want to hear any more about it."

Only the hum of the tires was heard for the next several minutes, and finally my mother turned on the radio to fill the void.

A Garden of Love

by

William B. Keller

Authors Choice Press

New York Lincoln Shanghai

A Garden of Love

Authors Choice Press
an imprint of iUniverse, Inc.

iUniverse books may be ordered through booksellers or by contacting:

iUniverse
2021 Pine Lake Road, Suite 100
Lincoln, NE 68512
www.iuniverse.com
1-800-Authors (1-800-288-4677)

Originally published by Commonwealth Publishing

ISBN-13: 978-0-595-00125-5 (pbk)
ISBN-13: 978-0-595-87379-1 (cloth)
ISBN-10: 0-595-00125-4 (pbk)
ISBN-10: 0-595-87379-0 (cloth)

Printed in the United States of America

This book is for Jill and Will.

Chapter 1

Life can be incredibly simple when you're thirteen years old, especially when you live in a rural Ohio community on a small farm. Certain things just flow along day to day with no thought of alteration or change. Things like cancer were what happened to other people; you know, the unspeakable 'C' word. That is, until that day.

We had recently moved into my parents' dream home, a ranch style with a huge living room and picture windows at the front and back. The two bedrooms were not that large. Remember this was what they wanted, not what was best for the re-sale market. My brother and I never even thought about having to share a room.

My mother liked the sandstone chimney out-side the house best of all. A large "K" was sculpted into the side, representing the Keller name. I learned to respect people's names thanks to my mother. Her name is Waneta, and she never hesi-tated to correct someone who attempted to mis-spell it as "Juanita". Had she gotten married as a young woman in the nineties, I am sure we would have known her as Waneta Mae Stoner-Keller.

I found her one afternoon studying the large K

with a critical eye. "Billy, come here for a minute." She either had forgotten that I had reached the age where "Billy" had become an abomination, Bill of course being the accepted more manly title, or like all the other adults in my life just chose to ignore my wishes. "Is that letter crooked?" Her eyebrows crinkled inward and the corners of her mouth grimaced downward in concentration.

"As a dog's back leg," I quickly replied. Of course that "K" was, in reality, the straightest and most perfectly balanced item in the universe but I didn't want to disappoint her.

She curled her short German fingers into fists which she shook at the unyielding chimney. "I knew it!" she shouted. Her eyes flashed at me in anger. "I swear that builder will tear this chimney down stone by stone and build this...this thing right."

For an instant I thought I had her. My mother would have died before a foul word would leave her mouth. That was just something that was "not done". Her resolve held, however, and her fists fell harmlessly to her sides.

"It's off to the right isn't it." This was a statement of fact, not a question.

"Oh no, Mom, it's way off to the left." I began to struggle in earnest now, the giggle tickling the back of my throat like a feather.

"What? It is?" Her head cocked to the side, eyes straining to see the tilt of the "K". She was so absorbed in this revelation that she forgot I was there. I prudently slipped away and continued playing, thinking no more about the incident.

Not having many neighbors results in an absence of playmates. My most constant companion was our dog, Daisy. She was a toy collie mix who didn't seem to mind the incredibly stupid name we had tagged her with. This name was a simple piece of fate, because Daisy's predecessor was a pretty mean dog named Nipper. Since Nipper lived up to her name, thanks to an electric company meter reader that unceremoniously kicked her out of his way when she was just a pup, we all thought that our next dog should be a "kinder, gentler" pet. (Sorry President Bush, my mother said it first.) Apparently it worked, because Daisy would not as much as chase a rabbit.

Daisy was incredibly flexible. She could run all day with me if I called her to play, but she was equally content to watch me for hours while I shot baskets in our driveway. My dad had bought a telephone pole which he planted at the edge of our double wide blacktop drive. He made a blackboard and centered a basketball rim ten feet up the pole. My father was an absolute genius when it came to making things. That rim was exactly ten feet to the inch from the pavement, and nothing less would do. I created my own basketball league, with myself of course as the star of one of the teams. I made up schedules and fantasy games for the league. When my team played another team on the schedule, I simply alternated shot for shot and played an imaginary game. I tried to make every shot, but I must admit I made more attempts from spots that I was not as good when the other team had the ball.

Daisy would sit and watch me play for hours at a time, happy just to be near me, and never once raising an occasional eyebrow when an opponent missed a long shot and then Keller rushed in for the rebound, drove the length of the court, and scored an easy jump shot. My games went to one hundred, and most were won by my team.

I was involved in a close game with only a few

points to go when my father's car came into the driveway. I was surprised because he was home early from work, something that just never happened. Whenever I saw him I had the illusion of looking into a mirror. My father had to admit, even though perhaps sometimes reluctantly, that I was his son, because we were virtually twins. Even when he was in his forties and me a young teen, some people at a distance could not tell us apart. I am about an inch taller than his five foot six inches, but nearly every other feature is identical. Although he is a quiet man, he always said a lot to me through his actions. My father did not hesitate, he moved with precision and confidence. Words were not as necessary because he knew what was going to happen, so why talk about it.

He pulled the car onto the gravel path that led to the barn so that he would not disturb my game. Daisy, of course, as all good family dogs do, went wild with glee and wiggled and fell all over herself. Dad waited patiently as she romped in front of the car, finally yielding so he could pull forward far enough to completely clear the blacktop. He knelt to scratch the dog's ears, and Daisy groaned in ecstasy.

"Hey, Bill," he said in his mild tenor voice. "Who's winning today?" he asked with a fond smile.

"The good guys of course," I said with equal fondness. I loved him even more for remembering to drop the dreaded "y" from my name. I was also quite amazed because I had never told anyone about my fantasy games, so I didn't know if Dad had figured out my secret or was just making conversation. I didn't really care if he knew because this was the last man on earth who would ever make fun of someone.

He went to the trunk of his car and got out an

old beat up lunch pail. I can't say that he used the same lunch pail for his whole working career, but I can remember only one. Dad worked at the Lima Locomotive Works, a company that in the old days made engines for the railroad. They converted to a heavy equipment manufacturer and my father read blueprints and created templates which were used as guides to make huge road construction machinery. Fortunately, he eventually reached retirement age before the plant closed permanently, and his pension and benefits were protected in escrow.

Retirement was the last thing on his mind that day. He quickly headed for the back door and paused for a moment to look back at me. "Do you know why your mother is so riled up about the chimney?" he asked. "I've got our builder on the way over and she says the chimney needs to be redone."

I gulped hard and tried to keep my voice level. "Well, I think maybe she doesn't like the "K" on the chimney." Hopefully he would think the sweat running down my face was all from playing basketball.

"That doesn't make sense" he muttered. "She loves that 'K'."

"Maybe you should ask her, Dad," I said hopefully. It worked because without another word he went inside, just as another car pulled into our drive. Ed Klingbeil, the builder who put up the house and did some of the finish work, brought his car clear up to the pole that my basket was hung from. I stepped aside, basketball tucked under my arm, and he jumped out of his car without so much as a glance my way. Ed Klingbeil was a jerk.

Daisy growled low in her throat, this being the only person in the world she did not like. I resisted the urge to tell her to bite him and took my now useless ball into the garage. I probably would have stopped the game anyway, because I strolled around to the back of the house to position myself to hear the fireworks. Daisy padded silently beside me.

My mother was shouting at Ed Klingbeil. Daisy's ears shot up and I put a hand on her head to calm her. After fifteen minutes of arguing I heard her say what I was silently praying I would not hear. "Billy even said it was crooked." Her voice rose another octave. "I kind of thought so but he convinced me." By now I was afraid a window would crack like in a Memorex commercial.

Daisy followed me as I tip-toed toward the other side of the house, but I froze when I heard my father call my name. I walked slowly around to the side of the house, approaching him slowly. I was giving him my best confused, "who me?" look. He wasn't buying any of it.

"Come around here and look at the chimney." His tone contained a command, not a request. He walked quickly through the grass and I kept up without a word. Daisy stopped to chase a Monarch butterfly, then quickly caught us, pushing a wet nose into my palm in a demand for a scratch on her head. I wiggled my fingers out of reflex.

We all stood looking at the sandstone chimney. I almost giggled as I thought, *Here we are staring at this thing like it's one of the giant heads on Easter Island.* The humor disappeared like a wisp of early morning fog when I realized that everyone was staring at me.

"Well, it is crooked," I blurted out, a prosecution witness melting in the heat of cross examination. "It leans way to the right."

"Wait a minute," my mother mused. "I said it

was leaning to the right before, and you said it leaned to the left." Her eyes narrowed as the realization hit home. "This thing is straight isn't it?" She was staring hard now.

"You and I will talk later," my father said in a low voice. He left out the "You're dead."

Chapter 2

After being grounded for a week, which is tough in the summer, I had a lot of catching up to do in my fantasy basketball league. That first week out of "Attica," as I called it to myself, my mother didn't help me to catch up. She went shopping for two days and she took me to my Aunt Edie's every day. This was far from punishment though, as I would never miss a chance to go.

My mother's sister and her husband, Eddie, (yes, Edie and Eddie), did not have children. Because my mother and Aunt Edie were very close, she could get away with being our second mom. "Waneta", Edie would say in her shrill voice to my mother, "those boys are like my own."

With a smile my mother just quietly acquiesced, she never being one to object to a showing of love to her boys. My brother Rick and I ate it up. We knew if there was any senseless, waste of money, piece of junk that we wanted, Aunt Edie was good for the cash. If food was what we needed, Uncle Eddie came into play. He understood the value of a full stomach and never in any circumstances denied food to us. My parents would have shot him, but he even gave us small glasses of beer when we asked for them. It tasted terrible but we enjoyed the adult feeling of doing something that a child should not do.

Visits to the Zelno's, Uncle Eddie was from an old world Polish family, were like Christmas every day for Rick and me. We took comic books and magazines with us to show Aunt Edie what we just had to have in the ads. My favorites were muscle building courses and my brother liked anything musical. Some of the things she bought us were so foolish that we all agreed without saying a word that the item would be delivered to and kept at the Zelno's, never mentioning the purchase to my mother and father. We were there enough, and most of the mail order purchases were such junk, that interest soon waned and, I presume, the treasures ended up in the trash.

We did earn some of the pampering. Aunt Edie insisted that we help her do some work around the house in return for her generosity. Today became a work day.

"Don't pull the flowers," my Aunt Edie was directing needlessly. She was watching me with a critical eye pull weeds from her treasured flower bed. "There. That one right there. Be really careful now." Her arms waved wildly in emphasis.

I glanced glumly toward the far end of the bed where Rick was working, pretending he wasn't watching me get the business. His turn would come, as she usually bounced back and forth between us like a pin ball. She usually directed more attention to me, probably because I was younger. We had agreed to clean the flower beds for tickets to the circus. We had two more days to finish the job before the show.

"Remember," Aunt Edie shook her finger for effect, "you have to finish this job or I won't buy the tickets." She gave her head a sharp shake to seal her words. "And don't slop your way through it and pull up half my flowers," she finished with a flourish.

Of course it was all nonsense. She bought the tickets the day they went on sale to guarantee the best seats for "her boys". Our goal was to stall the work long enough to escape as much toil as possible. It was a game we had played before.

"It sure is hot out here Aunt Edie," I complained. "When can we stop for a glass of lemonade?" I rubbed the sleeve of my shirt over my face as an exclamation point.

"I think ten minutes of work is not long enough to get a break," she growled. Well, as close as she could come to growling anyway. "This flower bed has got to be weeded."

My brother must have been too obvious in his malingering because the trim little pinball bounced toward him. "What's your holdup Ricky?" Oh heaven help me. Rick was four years my senior and he was still "Ricky". I'd be Billy in my fifties at this rate. "I guess I give you boys too much," she lamented.

Rick looked at her mournfully, frankly the work of a master in my humble opinion. "It sure is hot enough to pass out," he whined, maybe a bit too much but that was his call, not mine. He borrowed my sleeve over the forehead move, which I can't begrudge him because, after all, this was a team effort.

"Oh all right," Aunt Edie sighed. "Come on in the house and drink a glass of lemonade." She stalked toward the house but then abruptly stopped and turned on us, almost catching our silent celebration. "But I want to tell you right now, you've got to get right back out here or I'll give those circus tickets to the Children's Home," she barked.

"Yes, ma'am," we murmured contritely.

Mother picked us up that evening, finding both of us half sick from stuffing our faces all day in front of the television set. The flower garden remained untouched.

The day of the circus Aunt Edie picked us up without comment. She must have spent the equivalent of a week's pay on overpriced hot dogs, cotton candy, and assorted trash like pennants, shirts, official programs, and, of course, an elephant trunk hat for each of us. Rick and I were so embarrassed by the ridiculous hats that we didn't even wait until the end of the performance before we stuffed them into our pockets. Keeping the tradition of spoiling us like rotten fruit, Aunt Edie never complained once and simply bought what we asked for. I should mention too, that she paid for V.I.P. seats, which put us within inches of the animals as they came into the center ring.

"Can you believe this?" she said, her face flushed with excitement. "I could have touched that elephant."

"Yeah," I mumbled almost absently, my concentration distracted by my black, low cut canvas Converse All Stars. I had insisted on a pair because Bob Cousy of the Boston Celtics wore them. Most of the kids even called them Cousy's. Of course my Aunt had purchased them for me during our last trip to town. My attention was diverted because our elephant, as he passed by, had relieved his bowel. The result was a ten pound block of foul smelling mush that splashed onto my Cousy's, almost covering them.

My brother Rick almost went wild. I don't think I ever saw anyone laugh that hard in my life. Aunt Edie never even noticed, she was so excited about the circus. She never even realized that I went home barefooted, my socks and the defiled sneakers having been scraped up by a clown with a huge scoop shovel. Rick went on for months about my smelly feet.

Chapter 3

My mother and father are really great people. As I look back on those days I can't believe some of the things they put up with. Country kids pretty much run the township, and I could go as far as my bike would take me as long as I was home by lunch time and again for dinner. There was really not much to get into, because farm land stretched everywhere. The few neighbors that were in the area knew everyone and welcomed all the children that came by like they were family.

About a half an hour away by bicycle was a go-cart race track. Every Sunday after church Rick and I almost tore the buttons off of our dress shirts to save some precious moments. Lunch was eaten like two dogs biting off huge chunks of meat and swallowing it whole. My mother gave up trying to make us eat like humans on Sundays.

Entrance to the go-cart raceway was fifty cents, paid for by my parents. They also gave us an extra dollar each to buy snacks. I think they appreciated giving us something without Aunt Edie or Uncle Eddie saying, "Oh, we'll take care of it."

All of the kids in the area went to the Sunday races. We had some really close friendships that developed just from this one weekly summer activity. The most daring member of our group was Harold "Bud" Campbell. He was always elected to go to the concession stand and buy cigarettes. It wasn't that Bud was older or anything as simple as that, he was just nervier. Old Man Higgins ran the concession stand and would have sold the black plague if there was a penny in it for him. A two-year-old could have purchased a pack of smokes from that concession stand.

"Here you go guys," Bud said with an ornery, lopsided grin. "That'll be fifty cents."

"Come on, Bud" I complained. "They only cost thirty cents."

"Then go on up there and buy them yourself," he said flatly. "My price is higher than the concession stand. But go see Old Man Higgins. Tell him I sent you," he concluded with a wink. Bud was tall, thin, and very good looking. He is one of those people who can get away with anything. We all knew that if any of us walked up there and tried to buy cigarettes, a cop would appear out of nowhere (despite the fact we had never seen one at the races), and our next stop would be the front door of our home in handcuffs. Bud never worried about that, whether it was bravado or that he knew his parents didn't care, we didn't know. He was always the first one to throw a rock at a window, or prop a nail against the tire of a parked car. He prided himself on his fearlessness.

"Here you go," my brother growled. "But you know you're a thief," he added as the money exchanged hands.

Bud just chuckled as he handed over the pack of Marlboro's, the smoke of choice for the early teen crowd. And in the flip top box of course.

"Hey," I complained, "there's four missing."

"Well, I'll be a doggone do gooder," Bud exclaimed with false amazement. "I guess the Marlboro Man must have smoked a few at the plant. Maybe you ought to check and see if his horse dropped somethin' in there too." He pulled a Marlboro from his shirt pocket and lit it with an Ohio Blue Tip kitchen match that came from the corner of his mouth. His thumb nail was darkened from many match lightings in the past. He inhaled deeply and blew out the match with a breathy cloud of smoke.

I punched Ozzie Ramser on the arm as he peeked into the open cigarette box to check for horse droppings. Ozzie would have believed the *Wizard of Oz* was a true story if you told him it was so. "Don't be a dope, Ozzie," I said. "Bud's not being straight."

"Oh, yeah, sure," Ozzie quickly agreed, obviously not understanding what I meant. "Ol' Bud," he grinned, looking around at us to see if he had reacted properly.

"Come on, come on." Rick grabbed the cigarettes and shoved them into his pocket. "Let's go have a smoke." He strode off purposefully toward the outdoor toilet on the far side of the track.

Bud Campbell was the only one with nerve enough to smoke in front of adults. The crowd was there to enjoy a Sunday afternoon's entertainment and could not have cared less about some stupid little kids trying to play grownup, but our child's paranoia forced us to be secretive. We would crowd behind the old smelly outhouse that served both men and women, although I don't believe a woman ever went to the go-cart races. I also don't know what we thought we were hiding, because when out little group lit up and started puffing away, the smoke billowed up like the toilet was on fire. Everyone had to know what we were doing.

"This is great," I exclaimed between coughing fits.

"Great?" asked a boy whom I didn't even know. "You're about to choke to death."

"Yeah, well, that's because I'm inhaling so deep," I lied. Actually, I didn't inhale at all. It was just the smoke curling under my nose that gave me the problem.

"We do this all the time," Ozzie insisted, his eyes watering and nose dripping like a leaky gutter from the smoke.

This ritual was important to us because there was no other way most of us could get together but at the races. We all lived so far apart that bikes were not practical and, in fact, only Bud Campbell, Rick, and I could even get there on bikes. The rest of the boys came in cars with their dads or an older brother. We had a simple, four hour, one day per week summer friendship, and it meant the world to me.

"We ought to do something different today," said Stevie Noble, normally one of the quieter boys in our little group.

He got our attention immediately, new ideas being a welcome change. Bud, ever the leader, spoke first. "Let's hear it, Steve," he said. Bud never put the childish endings on names, the "ie" on Stevie, the "y" on Billy. He thought that was for babies, not mature, cigarette-smoking men like us.

Stevie savored the moment of our total attention. He slowly raised his small hands, palms down, until his fingers were spread like fans, each one pointing at us like stubby guns. "Let's send Bud up there to Old Man Higgins and get us some chewing tobacco." He quickly turned his palms in and brought them together quickly with a sharp crack. Ozzie jumped and blinked his eyes.

"Great idea!" my brother Rick exclaimed. "Billy and me will throw in a quarter." He nodded my way.

I frowned but said nothing because I wanted to try a chew myself, but I resented not being able to speak my own piece. Several of the boys pulled coins out of their pockets and we quickly totaled a dollar and ten cents.

"Will this do it, Bud?" Stevie asked anxiously.

Bud squinted, took a long, last drag of his Marlboro, and expertly flicked it with his thumb and index finger ten feet away from himself. "Why don't I just take this money up there and find out?" he drawled, enjoying becoming the center of attention. He stretched leisurely and straightened his shirt before walking away, doing a nearly perfect John Wayne swagger.

Minutes later he returned, his left cheek bulging with a wad of tobacco. He tossed the opened package, emblazoned with the profile of a bright red Indian, to Stevie. Bud spat a brown stream onto the ground and winked conspiratorially. "You're the idea kid, you get the first chew."

"Wow, Red Man," Stevie whispered reverently. He opened the package with trembling hands, then closed his eyes and sniffed deliciously. "Isn't that wonderful?" He took a pinch between thumb and index finger and stuck it into his mouth.

We passed the foil package around, each taking a turn at the sweet smelling tobacco. I was the first to throw up. I didn't swallow all of the juice like the stories you hear, but even though I spit again and again, a small amount of the dark liquid got swallowed. For a novice, small amounts are enough. This started a chain reaction. One by one the guys brought up the contents of their stomachs. The more we got sick, the sicker each person got. For years the whole township talked about how all the boys got food poisoning at the go-cart track. Everyone figured the only one who didn't eat that day was Bud Campbell because he was fine. They thought he sure acted odd though, the way he laughed at all of the boys who were sick.

Chapter 4

Sunday mornings meant our weekly visit to the Liberty Chapel Methodist Church. Unlike a lot of kids, I really enjoyed going to this rural house of worship. I thought the cemetery on the east side of the building was especially neat. Something about living your life in one area, going to church each week, and finally coming to rest close enough to hear the music coming through the open windows on Sunday mornings appealed to me even as a child. My mother and father usually agreed to leave home a half hour early so I could prowl about the eternal granite stones, never tiring of looking at the names and dates. Rick thought it was ridiculous but finally learned to put up with my eccentricities.

My mother couldn't always walk with me because she tended to cry. Cemeteries affected her that way. My father usually helped out in the church when we came early, and Rick liked to help out too, even though he would never admit it. So, often my Sunday morning visits with the dead were solitary, which didn't bother me at all. In fact, when I try to remember back to that time, I don't recollect any bad weather or even the cold, although I know I walked that cemetery every Sunday.

A truly fine group of people made up our congregation. Most were simple, hard working folks with hearts of gold. One of my favorites, Lucy Finmaster, was missing the tip of her index finger. How she lost it remains to this day a mystery, as she told a different story each time someone asked. My personal favorite went something like this:

"I was just shy of my eighteenth birthday," she said solemnly, looking around to make sure everyone's attention was where it belonged, which was on her. "My problem was I knew too much. You know, already a woman of the world, so don't try to tell me anything. That kind of smart." Lucy nodded her head in sagelike wisdom, assured that we must have all understood. "My daddy was the schoolmaster at the one room school over on route eighty one," she gestured in the general direction, "and he was one smart man. Some folks thought it was odd that a man was the school teacher, but since daddy could whip any man Jack son in Allen County, nobody said nothin' about it to his face."

Lucy edged her tiny frame toward the edge of her chair. She weighed well under a hundred pounds and stood just a touch under five feet, but I was a bit in love with her. Her red hair and light features reminded me of Lucille Ball in *I Love Lucy*. I used to greet her with, "Hi, I love Lucy." She would laugh and wink at me, and I would melt into the floor. I got to tell her that I loved her in an offhand way and got away with it. My young heart was thrilled.

"I used to tell people exactly what I thought of them," she was saying. "My daddy kept saying, 'Lucy, some day you're going to run into someone who won't take your mouth.' I never worried much about it though, because I always figured my daddy would just whip anyone who gave me trouble." She tossed her soft red curls for emphasis.

"Well, one day this boy who worked at the Lafayette grain elevator got fresh with me." She held her hand up, head cocked to one side in response to the gasp of us children for whom she was performing. "Now don't get me wrong," she clarified, there wasn't nothing wrong with what went on, he just leaned over and kissed me on the cheek."

"Thank goodness," I murmured, much to Lucy's delight.

"Well, I want to just go and tell you, I lit into him." Her hair bounced in emphasis. "I was screamin' and hollerin' and finally I just started to shake my finger at him." Her voice increased in volume as she warmed to the story.

"I told him my daddy would beat him to death for attackin' me, and boy would he be sorry." She paused now, looking at each one of us, making sure we were paying attention I guess. Taking a deep breath she continued in a low voice, so low that we had to lean in toward her to hear clearly. "Well, I kept wavin' my finger at him and finally that ol' finger, it poked him in the eye. Now, back in them days I had sharp nails. When I hit that boy's eye, it all but put it out. Without even blinkin' that eye he dropped his head and snapped his teeth like a dog and bit my finger off right at the joint." Lucy held up the digitless hand for us to see.

"Wha... what did he do with it?" one of the little kids asked her.

"Why, he swallowed it of course." Lucy finished triumphantly.

We all started yelling at the same time. Lucy just waited for the noise to die down, obviously enjoying our reaction.

"Did he chew it up?" I asked, the question

hushing our little group.

"No silly," she giggled, obviously appreciating the question. "He just gave a gulp and down his throat she slid."

Well, that got us going again. A couple of the youngest kids looked kind of green, and I knew there would be heck to pay if one of those kids threw up in church because of Lucy's stories.

"Now," she continued, moving forward with her story, "I was screamin' like a scalded cat. The boy run off and let me standin' there with the blood a pumpin' out of my finger."

The kid beside me gagged and I pushed him toward the door.

"My daddy took me to old Doc Hacook and he sewed the end closed. He didn't even use nothin' to stop the pain," she finished with pride.

Murmurs of "wow," "gee," "neat," and "shoot me" came from the kids. Was she telling us the truth? Well, she was missing a large part of that finger. The fact that this was the fifth or sixth time she had told us a different story about how she lost that finger seemed unimportant at the time.

"What did your daddy do to that boy?" I asked.

Lucy leaned forward and spoke in a conspiratory whisper. "That boy, he plum disappeared," she breathed. "Nobody knew where or what, nobody asked."

"Did your daddy kill him?" a little fellow asked. He was so engrossed that he didn't notice the saliva running from his mouth and dripping off his chin.

"I believe he did," she said firmly. "But he took it to his grave. I never knew for sure."

Someone had to break the spell, so I took the lead and said, "Dig for coal for us Lucy."

She put the stub of her finger up to her nose

and pretended to be deep inside. She scrunched up her face and said, "Wow, the coal is really deep today boys."

We screeched in delight and broke up the little group, talking about the horrors of not getting a finger bit off, but of swallowing one.

Our small church was too poor to afford a full time preacher, so we got not only divinity students, but we had to share them with the Lafayette Methodist Church. The two churches should have merged, but no one could agree which building would be used, so the two operated on their own. Because we got students we had a new preacher about once a year. My father complained that they looked like twelve year olds, even though I don't remember them looking too young. Many things happen that a kid hardly notices, but are really big deals to adults. I thought it was interesting to have different speakers from time to time. Some of them were really good, and others, well, they meant well.

One of the things that really worked up some of the people was the policy of the Methodist Church at that time of listing gift givers on a board in the front of the chapel. They didn't list the amount that each family gave, but they were ranked according to who gave the most money. For some, this became a contest. Now, I don't know if you've figured this out yet, but I really admire my mother and father. They made a conscious decision on the amount they would give and it in no way depended on the "tote board".

One evening my father came home after an unusually hard day at work. The telephone rang and he set his lunch pail down with one hand and answered the telephone with the other. It was the latest twelve year old preacher calling. I only heard one half of the conversation of course, but my father stood there after some preliminary pleasantries and just listened. The plastic handle of the telephone cracked loudly as he increased the pressure of his grip. All he did was thank the reverend for the call and said he would take care of the problem immediately.

Our telephone was one of those new designs that had a large round base with the dialer and disconnect button on the bottom. It looked like today's joy stick for a video game. My father slammed the telephone down and as neat as if he had hit it with a razor sharp machete, it fell into two pieces. "Waneta," he croaked. He was so angry, the bellow of rage didn't come out. "Waneta," he repeated, louder this time.

She came running into the kitchen, clearly alarmed. She looked at the broken telephone with an open mouth stare. "What on earth..." she began.

"That was the Reverend Fordwick," he growled. I swear it was Fordwick, just like the John Ritter character on the Waltons. I always believed he must have been patterned after our Reverend Fordwick. Maybe Earl Hamner was one of those little kids in our Sunday school class in those days. "He called to let us know," my father paused and leaned heavily on the kitchen bar stool, the anger making him tired, "that the Robinson's increased their giving. If we want to remain on the top of the list we have to increase our donation by ten dollars a week."

My mother looked like someone just told her that dinner was burned. "Well what did you tell him?" she sputtered.

"I said we'd take care of it," my father said triumphantly.

"But Kenneth, we agreed that our position on

that chart didn't mean a thing," she argued. "We give what we believe is right."

"I know that," he said with a wave of his hand.

"Then why did you tell Reverend Fordwick you'd take care of it?" she said with a perplexed look.

"What I meant by that," my father said forcefully, "was that we won't be attending a church anymore where the preacher is worried about who is number one on the gift list."

We began our search for a new church that very Sunday. Our first try was the Grace Gospel Living Word of Faith Tabernacle. After three lusty and exciting songs the preacher leaped to the podium and began screaming at all of us. Ten minutes later people all over the congregation started yelling and waving their arms. Suddenly a three-hundred-pound woman sitting next to me roared "Praise heaven" and fell across my lap. I began to scream at the top of my lungs from fear, although it immediately turned to pain. No one really noticed though because there were so many other people screaming and yelling throughout the congregation. My father had to pry me out from under the twitching and moaning woman, and we all ran for the exits. There was so much noise and jumping around that nobody even saw us leave.

The next Sunday we went to a little country chapel. We pulled into the gravel parking lot just as the back door opened. A man, I presume the preacher, wearing a pure white robe and white patent leather shoes came out and lifted his arms straight out to his sides, the loose material hanging down to make him look like a giant white bat.

"Hey look!" I exclaimed. "It's an angel."

My mom got so tickled that she couldn't get

control of her laughter. The more she laughed the more she got the rest of us laughing. We got so carried away that my father finally just took us home because we simply could not get under control.

The third time was the charm. We tried the Forest Park Evangelical United Brethren Church. A classmate from school saw us and offered to show me around. It was a nice, conventional Protestant church with lots of stained glass and a young, dedicated pastor. I walked into the sanctuary and looked past the rows of empty pews to the choir loft at the front of the church. There were about fifteen kids my age that made up the Sunday school class. Sitting on the end was the most beautiful girl with the most incredible blue eyes I had ever seen. My adolescent heart skipped a beat and then turned on the turbochargers. It beat so fast and so loud that I couldn't hear what my friend was saying as we walked forward.

My first thought was, *Someday I'm going to marry that girl.* My next thought was *You must be crazy, you're just a little kid.* Forgive me for jumping ahead, but I dated only four other girls for a total of about six months in my junior year of high school. Like Frankie Vali sang with The Four Seasons, "I only have eyes for you". My eyes and my heart from that day on belonged to that blue-eyed beauty, and my wonderful Jill one day became my wife during my senior year in college.

Chapter 5

Dollar days were sacred in the sixties. The prices were truly lowered to the point of being ridiculous, and it created a buying frenzy. Stores got together and agreed upon a date to lower prices on old stock and a few loss leaders, which got everyone to come to their particular store.

The Gregg's store in Lima once advertised a mink coat for two dollars to the first shopper that could find it hidden in the store. They caused a riot and created a situation that made me a family hero.

A huge crowd formed at the entrance of the store that morning. My mother and Aunt Edie were near the front of the mob because they left home at five o'clock that morning to be first in line. I was indentured to be a package carrier to enable the two determined shoppers to keep both hands free. This was the most effective way to sort through ten cent pocket books and one dollar sweaters. We were on the right side of the glass doors that fortunately opened inward, because as the crowd grew, its pressure slowly built and all of the early birds were being pressed against the door and the side of the building.

Precisely at nine o'clock in the morning two

store employees were sent out to unlock the doors. The hoard of people started to surge forward in anticipation before the keys touched the locks. The glass doors actually started to bow inward from the tremendous pressure. The now frightened employees hesitated in opening the groaning locks, making the people further back in the line think the doors must be opened and they were not getting in, so they pressed forward. A small woman to my right let out a small, strangled scream. She was pressed flat as a frog against the granite facade of the building and was turning a deep crimson.

"C...c...can't breathe," she gasped.

Without a thought I turned to face her and braced my hands on either side of her shoulders. My movement smashed me with bone cracking force against her body the instant another person was squeezed out of the way as a result of my push. I couldn't breathe either and was almost kissing her whether I wanted to or not. Pushing as hard as I could, I created a small space which enabled us to breathe.

With a loud splintering crack, the locks snapped, fortunately giving way before a glass door shattered, and the doors flew open. The two clerks turned and ran for their lives as the crowd flowed ahead like a tidal wave. I moved into the store without the benefit of my feet touching the floor. The woman I helped waved to me for an instant and then was lost in the crowd. My mother saw what happened and never forgot it. She has told half of the county about my heroism in saving that woman's life. I pretended that the whole thing was silly and not a big deal, but in reality I suppose I really did save that lady's life.

Inside the store it looked like a prison riot.

People were throwing clothes every which way and several fist fights broke out over who would get to buy a particular pair of shoes or earrings. My mother and Aunt Edie were pretty crazy shoppers, but they had too much class to fight over costume jewelry. Besides, they snatched up plenty of other bargains which kept me busy taking trip after trip to the car. I told them that next year we were bringing a pack mule. Aunt Edie noted that they already had one this year. Ha ha. Or should I say hee haw.

The department store was a mess, with more items on the floor than on the tables. Sales clerks developed that panicked, animal fear look in their eyes, the kind that a deer has when the headlights of your car catch them. The store put Lima on the national news with what happened next. There was a screech that came from the men's department when someone found the mink coat buried in a rack of suits. This woman held her treasure high in the air and whooped like an Indian warrior holding a settler's scalp.

Not more than five seconds had ticked by from the time of her discovery when six women soundlessly pounced on her and in an instant a mink coat tug of war began. Several more people, one a small man in a business suit, joined the battle. With a wrenching rip the coat virtually exploded into at least twenty pieces. The small band of attackers disappeared as fast as they had appeared, leaving the original claimant sprawled on the floor, surrounded by small pieces of fur.

The network news sources reported that five lawsuits were filed over the "Gregg's Dollar Daze" as it became known, and Paul Harvey added it to his "For What It's Worth" segment. All suits were settled out of court, but the only one which re-

ceived any notoriety was the lady who found the
fur coat. She was given another to replace the prize
she had found, and the two dollar price was waived.
My father always believed that was the only suit
which was ever really filed. He was convinced that
the rest were invented by an eager press corps.
Either way, Gregg's Department Store never par-
ticipated in the annual Dollar Days Sale again.

We traditionally celebrated the many bargains
with a stop at the Kewpee, the absolutely best
hamburger shop in the U.S. and the world. Their
logo was, and is to this day, a Kewpee doll with its
cute smile, pot belly, and diaper. They served the
burgers in a paper wrapper with the Kewpee doll
in the center and the phrase, "Hamburg with a
pickle on top, makes your heart go flippity flop.
Kewpee Hotels." If there was a real Kewpee Hotel
no one had ever heard of it nor could they remember seeing a hotel by that name. I don't know what
it meant. Probably because no one else knew either.
    The founder of the Kewpee, Spud Wilson, lived
in the Lima area all of his life. A favorite joke in
town was, "Hey! Did you hear they found Spud
Wilson in his basement with the gas on?" "Oh no,
what happened?" was the hoped for reply from the
one person in town that had been in an asylum or
prison or something and did not know the joke.
"Nothing. He was just cooking Kewpees." This was
considered the best clean joke in town.
    There were five items for sale at the Kewpee.
Cheeseburgers, fries, chili, pie, and malts in the
old fashioned, tall, thick frosted dishes. Coffee or
soft drinks were free in the old days if you bought
anything else. A legend began that claimed someone had put L.S.D., a favorite drug of the Timothy

Leary set, into the salt shakers. Supposedly a bunch of high school kids went wild from the stuff and by the time the story was around for several years it had expanded to two people dropping dead in the back booth after experiencing a very bad trip. Another nonsense story of course, but the Kewpee actually had to replace the salt and pepper shakers with the little tear open individual packets which they use to this very day.

The big deal was the drive through. Three girls ran out to take orders from cars that pulled into the smallest space I've ever seen. The lead car pulled up to a fence at the edge of the restaurant's property. When their order came out in its white paper bag with the Kewpee baby already turning color from the hamburger grease, the car was turned to a right angle on a rotating cylinder, like a lazy Susan, built into the pavement. The customer was then in position to drive down an alley which led to North Street. This method was used for years until finally the gears that turned underground to move the circle of pavement broke. No one could be found to repair them, so the restaurant had to buy the building next to it, tear it down, and create a turn around and parking lot. The drive in was not so much fun after that.

The girls that worked as carhops all had lavish beehive or bouffant hairstyles, because Spud Wilson paid for a weekly trip to the beauty salon. Just to show how things have changed, the carhop job at the Kewpee was considered one of the better in the city for a young girl because of the fringe benefit trips to the beauty parlor. They weren't even paid in those days, their only income being tips.

My mother was talking excitedly about the bargains of the day and I was taking the greasy bag of burgers through the back window. This was a grownup thing for some kids, taking charge of the sack of food, but I just wanted first crack at my cheeseburger special. As our family car, approximately the size of a small third world country, turned on the blacktop lazy Susan, Aunt Edie groaned and bent over in her seat.

"Edith!" my mother said sharply. "Edith, what's wrong?" There was more curiosity than fear in her voice.

"Pain," Edie gasped. "Pain in my stomach." She groaned again.

The next car in line honked for us to get moving as we were in position to pull away. Mother jumped and put the car into gear. As she pulled slowly away, Edie groaned again and lay down, curled up in the fetal position on the front seat.

I leaned over the seat to see what was going on and my mother touched Edie's shoulder with her right hand and steered the car with her left. "Edith." Mother's voice was tight, frightened now. "What on earth is going on." This was not a question but a comment.

"Doc Hacook," she sighed and then sat up. "I'm going to have to see Doc." The color was returning to her cheeks and she seemed to be just fine.

"You just scared me half to death," my mother chastised. "Are you sick Edith?" I could tell she was still worried because she continued to use "Edith".

"I don't know," she said with honesty while smoothing her hair back into place. Her hands trembled. "Once in a while I have this terrible pain in my stomach. Or maybe it's more like my back. You know, kind of in between." She sighed, a wry smile on her lips that did not travel up to her eyes. I could tell that she was frightened.

"How long has this been going on?" my mother inquired.

"Oh, a month or two," Edie replied guiltily. She

glanced over the back seat at me, the forgotten bag of Kewpees dangling from my left hand. I immediately felt like an intruder.

"And you haven't been to the doctor yet?" my mother snapped, more angry at her fear than her sister. I noticed her knuckles were white as they gripped the steering wheel.

"Well, for goodness sakes," she gave a wave of a still trembling hand, "you don't run to the doctor with every little thing. It costs money to just find out that nothing's wrong."

The car pulled abruptly to the curb, causing a blast of the horn from an angry driver behind us and pitching me to the opposite side of the seat. My mother slammed the car into park and turned sideways in her seat. She grabbed both of her sister's hands and pulled her toward her. Their faces almost touched, and Aunt Edie looked shocked. I slid down in my seat, wishing I were somewhere else. "Edith, tomorrow morning you and I are going to the doctor."

"Tomorrow's a work day," she protested.

"Tomorrow is not a work day." This was a command. "Tomorrow is a visit to Doc Hacook."

Mother's look left no room for argument. She was pulling so hard on Aunt Edie's arms that I was afraid she might hurt her. She held her for almost ten seconds to make sure that there were no arguments before gently loosening her grip. Both women had tears in their eyes.

The drive home was long and silent. The burgers were forgotten and lay on the floor of the car. When we arrived at the Zelno's, my mother and Aunt Edie hugged, they both cried again, and she got out of the car.

"I'll pick you up at eight in the morning," Mother reminded her. She backed out of the drive before anything more could be said.

Chapter 6

Doc Hacook was a classic rural doctor. He made house calls at all hours and refused to make appointments for office visits. It was strictly a first come, first served basis. I'm not sure if he ever locked the office. The earliest I was ever there was six a.m. and five people were already waiting. Three were snoring so loud they could have collectively caused hearing damage.

I'm sure people went to other doctors in the Lima area, but I don't believe I've ever known any. Doc was perhaps the fattest man I have ever seen. The man had no lap. The only small thing he possessed was a pencil thin mustache that was almost obscured by thick lips and a huge nose. My father used to say, "My gosh, even his nose is overweight."

Doc Hacook would have worked in a third world torture chamber if he could have made a living there. Whether or not it was intentional made little difference, but this man hurt people. My mother once almost had her finger smashed in a farm accident. Doc looked at the mangled mess and without so much as a bullet to bite on he cut away pieces of damaged finger. My mother almost passed out and the waiting room nearly emptied from the sounds of her scream. She said in later years that was the most barbaric treatment she had ever received.

My most famous Doc Hacook story happened when I was five. I became constipated and could not go to the bathroom, or do a number "two" as we used to say. After several days of this my mother called the Doc. He came to my Grandma Stoner's house, because that way he could check her blood pressure and cure my constipation with one visit. I was sitting on an old chamber pot on the back porch, trying desperately to move my bowels into action. Doc Hacook waddled up to me and looked down. At first I thought there was an eclipse or that I had been sitting there all day and it was now nightfall, but then I realized it was just Doc blocking the sun.

"Well, what have we got here?" he wheezed. "Why aren't you being a good little boy and going to the bathroom for your mom?" His eyes disappeared when he smiled so I wasn't sure that he was actually looking at me.

"I don't know," I said in my tinny five year old voice. "I just can't do number two and my belly hurts." My lower lip pushed out for emphasis.

"Well now," Doc said, his voice calm and soothing, "do you see what I have in my hand?"

His hand held a large bar of Ivory soap, fresh out of the wrapper. "Soap," I simply replied.

"Right," Doc said slowly. "It's soap." He leaned down closer to me, or as close as his stomach would permit, and shook the bar slowly. If he lost his balance and fell on me, I would have been smashed flat as the proverbial pancake.

Suddenly he grabbed me off of the pot and turned me upside down. He held me up close to his fat face, the smell of garlic almost making me throw up. "When I sit you back down on that pot, you've got two choices." His words growled like a savage dog. "You go to the bathroom right away or I'll soap your butt so it falls out." He flipped me over and slammed me onto the pot without another moment's hesitation.

I'm sure we've all heard the expression "that scared the ____ out of me". Well, that is precisely what happened. Doc Hacook stood over me with his arms folded across his chest and glared down like a hostile genie. The Enola Gay didn't cause any bigger explosion than what erupted from the force of my bowels. When I was done I looked up past his huge stomach, trying to see his eyes. I prayed that I had produced enough to satisfy him and that the soap would not be used.

Doc smiled and slid the bar of Ivory into his pocket. "Well, there we are now. Isn't that better?" He strode away to take my grandmother's blood pressure. I heard him say to my mother, "He was just being stubborn, there's nothing at all wrong with him. If he tries that little stunt again just tell him I'll be back." Even to this very day, as an adult, I have to close and lock the bathroom door to successfully do a "number two". When I served in the military at Fort Lewis in Washington State I had to go into the latrine after everyone else was asleep, because the long row of toilets had no privacy.

Despite his cruelties, Doc Hacook knew his business. My mother told me that when I was a newborn, I had what was commonly known as the three-month colic. Basically, a baby with colic cries every moment he or she is awake for the first three months of life. Almost at the turn of the page for the beginning of the fourth month, the constant crying goes away and life returns to normal. It was so bad that my mother couldn't take me to church because of the racket. Also, as you can imagine, her nerves were pretty well shot.

The most common treatment in those days was a mixture that included codeine. The kid ended up stoned for three months, and maybe susceptible for life to a drug problem. I personally believe this was the cause of the hippie movement of the sixties. All of the people who had colic as babies tried marijuana and said, "Wow man, this is, like, you know, great." It was really the once an addict always an addict philosophy kicking in. Their brain remembered how it felt as an infant to be stoned and they were easy to hook. Every person at Woodstock had been a baby with colic. Check it out.

Doc Hacook was, in regard to drugs, ahead of his time. He only treated colic in the most extreme of cases. "The crying only lasts for about three months," he would growl. "Just put up a calendar and mark off a day at a time. It will be over before you know it. You sure don't want your baby to be a drug addict."

He would come by our house and my mother would be half dead from lack of sleep and bad nerves. Doc would take me from her and drop into the beautiful cherry wood rocker that my grandfather made for her so that his grandchildren "could be rocked like they're supposed to." That cherry wood must have been tougher than metal because it made some horrible cracking sounds but never collapsed under Doc's enormous weight. He would plop me on top of his stomach and I instantly quit crying. Doc would fall almost immediately to sleep because he ran on about two hours sleep each night, and my poor mother sat on the edge of her chair, waiting for her baby to fall off of this mountain that heaved up and down as Doc snored.

After about fifteen minutes, Doc would jump and wake up, the movement bouncing me about a foot into the air and making my mother add to her gray hair collection. I would plop back down on Doc's belly and sink in several inches, totally unharmed. "Well," old Doc would rumble with a wide yawn, "there's absolutely nothing wrong with this baby. He no more has the colic than I."

He would be in his car in two minutes, preaching the whole time about drug addict babies. My mother said I would wait until his car actually disappeared over the hill to resume my crying. This went on night and day until I was three months old. At my ninety first day of life, I stopped crying and was, like magic, just like any other baby.

We sat in the big waiting room in the chairs with the leather seats and straight wood backs. I believe that Old Sparky, the name of the electric chair at the Ohio Penitentiary, might have been slightly more comfortable than Doc Hacook's chairs. The worst thing for me was his clock on the wall. It was slightly larger than Big Ben, and a huge pendulum ticked off the endless seconds. If the Chinese would have visited Doc Hacook's waiting room and listened to that tick tock, tick tock, they would have never needed to invent the water torture.

No one makes a sound in a doctor's waiting room. I always felt like I had been sent to the principal's office and was waiting for the bad news. Doc's secretary would break the silence by sticking her head through the door and saying, "Next." She was always quiet and never raised her voice, but I still always jumped. Another thing that I hated was that no one exited through the front door. A back exit to the office was used for anonymous getaways. It was as if someone who went into the examination rooms never came out. This was indeed an unsettling feeling.

"Next." It was the soft spoken nurse. Everyone in the room jumped. Aunt Edie took a deep breath and stood, her turn at long last. I had never seen an argument in the waiting room, like someone claiming that they were actually next in line. I've seen people in Doc Hacook's waiting room who looked close to dead, but no one ever entered out of turn.

My mother jumped to her feet and went in with her, this move causing some raised eyebrows for an instant, because traditionally the long walk through the exam area door was done alone. The thought was probably not one of concern for someone who was very sick, but instead one of suspicion in wondering who was trying to ditch into line.

My instructions were to wait, so I stayed planted in my uncomfortable chair and listened to that horrid clock tick. Minutes were like eternity on a normal day, and on this one I waited for one hundred twenty of them. With a loud scrape, the front door of the office waiting room finally opened. Instead of a new patient, it was my mother, motioning for me to leave. She had obviously left by the rear door after Aunt Edie's exam and walked back around to the entrance to retrieve me. The sacredness of the rear exit was maintained. Only I was the infidel by walking out of the waiting room through the entrance door. I'm not sure it had ever been done before, and under any other circumstances it could have been the highlight of my young life.

Aunt Edie was waiting in the car, her face ashen and drawn. Not a word was spoken when my mother and I crossed the fifty feet to the curb. I knew better than to utter a sound. After the car moved into traffic and we were on our way toward home, my mother reached over and patted her sister's hand.

"Edith, Doctor Fleckner is the best surgeon in the city. He's going to help you. Besides, he may say it's nothing." Her voice sounded hopeful.

"Doc Hacook is never wrong." Aunt Edie's voice was a whisper, so I leaned forward to hear better. My mother's backwards look flashed a warning and I sat back in my seat. "I'm going to die."

"No you are not," my mother flashed angrily. "You are absolutely not going to die and I don't want to hear any more about it."

Only the hum of the tires was heard for the next several minutes, and finally my mother turned on the radio to fill the void.

Chapter 7

I guess because I was just a kid I forgot about that visit to the doctor's office over the next few days. My mother and father talked in whispers for a few minutes that day and that seemed to be the end of it. Rick didn't seem to know anything at all, although we wouldn't have talked too much right then anyway because we were feuding.

Being a little brother is positively a ride into Dante's inferno. Older boys were more mobile, sporting new drivers' licenses and noisy, rust-infested junker cars. That summer changed my brother from an equal into a man. He could go to friends or they could come to our house. I was an instant fifth wheel, a fish bone caught in the throat.

Our cousin Joe now lived close enough to come visit since he could drive. The last thing he and Rick wanted was a little kid hanging around. For my part, I wanted to be as obnoxious as possible and force them to take me places. Since neither of them could ever afford gas money the grownups made such decisions for all of us as they handed over five dollars to fill the tank. This bribe of self tolerance got me an occasional drive-in movie or a trip to the root beer stand, but it did not get me a welcomed acceptance.

Our current feud was not, interestingly enough, over a car, but a bicycle. Rick and Joe decided to take a bike trip from our house to the other side of Lima. I'm not really sure what their motivation was and I still am not to this day aware of their plans, but I don't believe they just wanted to take a fun bike ride. My obligation, of course, was to make sure I could go along and ruin their day. The setup was boringly simple, with mother making it too easy to be a challenge. I must imagine she was not too keen about this little trip in the first place, and saw me as a convenient way to tame down the plans. The whole thing started like this:

"Mom," I whined. "I want to go on a bike ride too. Will you go with me?"

My mother would go on a bike ride about as soon as she would volunteer to experience labor pains. She patted me on the head and said in her best placating voice, "If you want to go on a bike ride honey, just ride to Grandma's, visit a bit, and then come home. She'll be glad to see you."

"But Mooom," (turn up the volume now) "that's only about a mile. I want to go on a long ride like Rick and Joe." I turned calf eyes on my brother who instantly got the message.

"No way," he flatly answered. "We're going to ride hard and fast and we don't want some short winded, stubby-legged kid holding us up." He looked at Joe who nodded silent approval.

"Short winded," I flared. "I'll ride you into the ditch, buster." He almost got me. If I spouted off too much Mother would turn on me and make me stay at home for punishment. With an instride recovery I shifted my gears back to, "Mooom."

"Ricky, why shouldn't your brother ride along with you boys? You two don't do enough together." She was swung so far my way there could be no turning back now.

Well, Rick's mistake was one made because of his youthful inexperience. Kids don't know how to think like parents, thank goodness for the sake of parenthood. Kids make statements that make total sense to them, but to adult parents could never be deemed acceptable. With a gleam of triumph in his eye, Rick blurted, "He's too small. He'll never be able to keep up." He thought his logic was infallible.

"Then I guess you'll just have to go slower," came the obvious parental answer. "You three boys have a good time." Eureka, discussion ended.

She gave each of us, including Joe, a dollar for lunch. My goodness that woman was brilliant! Joe would have backed out of the trip without that bribe. Parents are not even in the same universe as kids when it comes to savvy. Kids don't have a prayer, and they don't even realize it.

There was nothing more to say; I was in. The interesting thing is I didn't really want to go. Riding all day with two testosterone challenged older boys who currently were angry enough at me to bury my remains in a peat bog did not appeal to me in the least, but the victory was worth the inconvenience. I tried my best to not strut as we left the house, for fear of Mother changing her mind if she caught me.

"You may be going along," Rick snarled as soon as we got outside, "but you're not with us. Keep your trap shut and don't bother us. If you get tired that's your problem. Don't expect anyone to wait for you."

"Oh, wow!" I mocked. "This is so scary you know." I shrank back and covered my face with my hands, spreading my fingers so that I could see. I included a loud laugh just to complete the dig.

"Jerk," Rick mumbled, reaching for his bike.

"Dork," I mumbled in return.

"You guys are both idiots," Joe included, shaking his head. "The whole reason we didn't drive today was to not have to take you along for crying out loud. Now we have to ride bicycles all day instead of being there in an hour. Now let's get going or we'll get home after dark."

That ended the argument for the moment and we started down the blacktop drive. The next ten minutes were wasted chasing Daisy back home. She was excited when we got on our bicycles and saw an opportunity for a trip. Of course we couldn't take a three legged dog on an all day bike trip, she would never be able to stay with us. After a lot of yelling, and when Daisy's feelings were sufficiently hurt, she gave up the chase and we were at last on our way.

I'm proud to say I kept up pretty well. Of course Rick and Joe bent to the task at hand, peddling for all their young legs were worth. If they could make me give up in the first mile or two, Rick could send me packing without a reprisal from home. I believe my heart would have burst before I'd have given up that day. My lungs were on fire and my legs ached like an old man, but on and on they pistoned. My forehead touched the cool metal of my handlebars as I cut the wind resistance to a minimum. With my eyes focused on the pavement, I would have run over anything in my way and probably would have crashed if there was a curve in the road.

Joe grunted and went into a coast at long last, his fatigue more important to him than getting rid of me. Rick barreled on for fifty yards or so before coasting to a stop. I gratefully let up the moment I knew Joe gave in, as Rick wasn't going to dump him. I tried, unsuccessfully, to control my breathing in a macho show of strength. What actually happened was I nearly passed out from holding my breath. My already oxygen starved body thought I had died or was drowning or something. My stupid stunt left me gasping and wheezing louder than normal.

"You going to die?" Joe gasped, probably not much better off than I.

"Someday," I croaked, proud that at least my smart alec wit still was in working order.

"Come on, let's get moving," was Rick's labored contribution.

We took off again, still moving quickly but at a more reasonable pace. I was still pushed hard though, so most of my time was spent leaning over my handlebars and peddling for all I was worth. I kept up, but frankly had no idea where I was going because all I could see was pavement.

About an hour into our trip, which included turns and twists galore, my bike suddenly dropped in speed and began peddling like a stone. "Hey!" I yelled and sat up straight as an arrow. I quit laboring and nearly pitched off the front of my bike as it screeched to a stop. One backward glance told the story, my rear tire was flat.

After all of the smart kid comments like "just drive on the round side" and "you'll have to ride it like a clown does a unicycle" from Rick and Joe, we all settled down to come to a sensible conclusion. Oh, did I say sensible? How foolish can I be? The decision was really the only one ·possible for kids to come up with. The strong survive, the weak do not.

"You'll have to walk your bike home," Rick said without emotion.

"I can't do that," I argued. "I don't even know where I am."

"What?" Rick retorted angrily. He had that "oh for crying out loud what a totally stupid idiot" look on his face. "How can you have ridden all this way and not know where you are." It was a statement, not a question.

"Because you butt breath's went so fast I couldn't keep up without leaning over and peddling as fast as I could." Of course including Joe in my butt breath comment lost me any possible sympathy I might have hoped for from him. "All I've been able to see all morning is pavement and white lines."

"Well," Joe said slowly, "then I guess you've got a problem." The key word here was you instead of we. "Here's what you do," and he fires off a list of directions that lost me two streets into his instructions.

"Wait a minute." My protest was weak because my confidence was sinking faster than the Titanic. "I didn't get all of that." Darn it, my voice had a tremble in it.

"How many times do you need to hear it?" Rick snapped. He repeated the same general instruction, except twice as fast. "Come on Joe, let's get going," he finished, almost in one breath. Without another word or as much as a backward glance, the two older boys mounted their bicycles and were off.

I was so shocked that I couldn't speak. If there would have been an audience, I could have cried, but since I was alone I didn't bother with the wasted effort. I just stood beside that country road and stared at them until their bikes disappeared over a rise. A car roaring down the narrow pavement woke me from my lethargy and I took an additional step backward as small stones and grit blew into my face.

There really was nothing to do but start walking and pushing my disabled bike. A bicycle with a flat tire will move, but it's kind of like pushing it through wet cement. Besides it being a warm day I was really working hard. Sweat ran in dirty rivulets down my face. I was soon tired and thirsty and, of course, hopelessly lost. Then I did the absolutely unforgivable guy thing, I started to cry. I know it was a delayed reaction from when Rick and Joe first abandoned me, but I was still ashamed. Along with the shame came despair, then followed fear, and finally fatigue.

I followed the route as close to the directions I had been given as was possible, and I would imagine that I made several wrong decisions at the intersections encountered. The blasted bike was killing me, but how could I abandon the most valuable possession a boy ever owns? Push on. Don't quit. Be brave. Take another step. What a bunch of baloney.

Country roads have houses far and few between, especially when one is on foot. I finally saw one, but I hesitated to ask for help. Even in the early sixties parents spent half of their lives warning children to avoid strangers. Because they can't think of everything, there's no exception granted for a boy with a flat tire and two idiot companions who gleefully dump him in the middle of nowhere. It was a small house, almost a cottage really, that had come into view as I trudged along. I remember thinking of Hansel and Gretel approaching the pretty little gingerbread house. This little place could have been the model. It wasn't food that I wanted, it was water. I never thought I could get this thirsty and still be alive. Swallowing was close to impossible as there was just no moisture in my mouth.

All country homes have outside faucets, usually connected to a well. Nasty things like iron deposits and the rotten egg smell of black sulfur were common, but I would have drank a glass of pond water full of tadpoles right at that moment. I dropped my bike at the edge of the road and walked down the long stone drive toward the front of the house. I debated as my tennis shoes made crunching sounds in the gravel whether I should go to the door. Fear, shyness, or a combination of the two talked me out of this option. Besides, who would care if I took a drink of water from their faucet?

A pit bulldog, probably named Buster, cared a lot. The outside faucet turned out to be at the back of the house, another common occurrence, so I had to walk around the house until I found it. There was a dog house tucked away at the rear of the dandelion covered lawn, but I needed water so badly I hardly noticed. The faucet made a loud squeak when I turned it, and tepid water flowed immediately, full of rusty flakes from the seldom used pipes. I allowed the wonderful, wet outpouring to drown a small Canadian thistle growing nearby, hoping to flush out the rust and get cooler water to drink.

I finally cupped my hands and drank, dirty hands and all. It seemed like I swallowed gallons of water before I stopped, my stomach sloshing and bulging. The loud squeak repeated itself when I turned off that wonder flow of water. I sighed and stood , ready to again face the rest of my trek home, wherever that was. Buster, as he will always be known to me, was standing quietly nearby watching me. He had walked to within ten feet of me and stood poised to strike, like a statue placed among the dandelions.

My first reaction was to smile. I like dogs and they normally are friendly to me. Remember the cute little dog with the bulls eye on his face in The Little Rascal series? Buster looked exactly like that dog. He was really quite adorable. "Well, hello there," I began with a smile, and the dog attacked. His teeth peeled back with a snarl and his powerful legs shot him forward.

A rose trellis with a half dead rose bush wound through it beside the faucet. Without an instant of thought I grabbed it and climbed, not feeling the thorns that tore at my skin and pulled my clothes. The trellis reached the edge of the roof and I scrambled on top of the house before looking down at the angry dog. He was jumping up and down in a total frenzy, stopping from time to time for a bite at the rose trellis. After a few minutes he bit through the thin wood and the rose bush did not have the strength to hold it up. In slow motion the whole thing sank in a crumpled heap to the ground.

I figured my only way down was to hang from the gutter and drop, which actually was not that far to fall. The problem remained that the dog was sure to rip me apart the moment I hit the ground. Dogs don't have much staying power. "Buster" soon got tired and sat down, staring at me with patient interest. I suddenly figured out that if I was to get off of this roof, I had to keep the dog from resting. Scrambling to my feet, I ran to the peak of the roof, paused a moment, and then moved to the front edge. I sat down and carefully peered onto the front lawn, waiting for the dog to come around the corner. Buster was moving so fast when he came around to the front of the house that he lost footing and rolled over twice before landing on all four feet. He barked angrily and ran in circles, venting his fury.

Finally he set down, sides heaving and tongue lolling out like a pink slab. Instantly I scrambled to my feet and went back over the roof to the back of the house, where I was joined a moment later by the dog. Back and forth we went for nearly an hour, with the dog slowing a bit more with each trip. Finally, he stopped in the back yard and did not follow when I scrambled over the roof to the front of the house. Still, I was not satisfied. He had to be so tired that the sound of me jumping down would not give him a burst of energy and resolve. "Buster" I yelled, and he came running at the sound of my voice. I knew when I finally had him, because he finally just trotted back to his dog house, head hanging in defeat, and disappeared inside. I didn't wait for a moment. Scrambling to the front of the roof, I grabbed the gutter and swung to the ground. I ran to the road without looking back, crossed the hot surface to my bike, and then I looked back. There was no dog.

I resumed my walk toward...home? I didn't know where to go, so I just walked as quickly as my bike permitted. Close to dusk I was about to give up. I had not seen one person in a front yard or a car on the road. Call it the ignorance of youth, but I could simply not make myself knock on a door. I was more afraid of that unknown than I was of my reality. I did see a friendly looking farm house in the distance, and I decided to make it my next goal. Hunger was snarling at me almost as loud as the pit bull, and I was thirsty again. My feet were blistered, my skin sunburned, and my arms ached from pushing my bicycle. I had reached way beyond my limit.

I saw a man working on a tractor in front of his barn, and I knew I was going to be all right. I would call home and ask my parents to come for me. I dropped my bike at the edge of the dirt path leading to the barn and trudged tiredly up to the farmer. His back was turned and I could hear him cursing softly as he worked on an aged John Deere tractor. "Excuse me." My voice was hoarse from thirst, dust, and fatigue.

The man started slightly and turned toward me, holding an open end wrench in a work scared hand. "Well I'll be darned," he said with a smile. "What brings you here, Billy?"

My mouth fell open in shock. It was Lee Fore, my school bus driver. "Wow," I said stupidly. "Hi Mr. Fore." Then I just stared at him, grinning like a tourist visiting a foreign country.

"Are you all right son?" Mr. Fore said, a puzzled look on his face. "You look like you've been through the old mill."

"Oh, uh, yeah," I stammered. "My bike broke down."

"Well shoot," Mr. Fore said sympathetically, "you'd probably like a ride home."

"I sure would," I cried, much too eagerly.

"What are you doing this far from home?" he asked as we walked toward my damaged bike. He probably noticed how terrible I looked. "I'm surprised your folks will let you go this far."

Since I had absolutely no idea where I was, I did not know how to answer him. "Well, I was with my brother and my cousin Joe." Why not try the truth. "When my tire went flat they went on and I started for home."

"What made you boys decide to come out this way?" Mr. Fore asked. "Were you headed for Columbus Grove?"

"Well, yes, I guess so." Okay, not the whole truth. "They didn't really tell me where they were going, they just, well, went."

His eyebrows knitted closer together. "Ummmm, I see." He lifted my bike with ease and carried it to the back of his ancient Chevrolet pickup truck. He opened his mouth to say something, then just shrugged and gestured to the cab of the truck. "Climb on in."

I was never so grateful to sit down in my life. I watched where he drove, trying to keep track of the turns and distance, and was soon lost again. Finally I saw the Bluelick Road sign and knew I was home free. We pulled into our driveway and my mother came running out the side door, a dripping wet dish in one hand and a Brillo soap pad in the other. Lee said very little as he unloaded my bike, only that he gave me a lift because my tire was flat. After many thank yous from my mother and another from me, he went on his way. I figured I was dead, but Mother just hugged me.

"Your brother is grounded for life," she growled.

"Why Mom?" I said. "It just took me a while to walk home." I didn't want to admit that I had been lost. "A dog chased me or I would have been home sooner."

Not one more word was said about my ordeal, and Rick was off the hook. He didn't know why I helped him out of the mess, but he let it go too. I have no other explanation for my mercy except to say that sometimes, a person just has to take the high ground.

Chapter 8

Aunt Edie went into the hospital on a gray, ugly day. Rain came and went, not seeming to know what was the right thing to do. Everyone was a basket case, from my mother to Uncle Eddie. The whole attitude fed on itself like a pack of hungry wolves. I probably didn't really understand the gravity of the whole thing, but I sure felt the tension.

One person was not the least bit upset, at least outwardly. Aunt Edie had said barely one word; she just sat there somberly watching everyone else act like idiots. Apparently I didn't appear very excited either because she came over to the hard plastic covered sofa in the hospital admitting area where I waited and plopped down beside me. Her stomach was so swollen a bystander would have presumed she was there to deliver a baby. A bizarre thought floated into my mind that if I stuck her with a pin, the poison gas would escape harmlessly into the atmosphere, her belly would deflate, and we could all go home.

I looked into her eyes and saw pain. I was too young to understand it, but I could tell all was not as it should be. Not knowing what to say I murmured, "I love you Aunt Edie."

Tears pooled into her eyes and I thought my comment must have been a mistake. Then without a word she pulled me close and planted a sandpaper dry kiss on my cheek. She swallowed hard and licked her lips, showing again the signs of her fear. "Everyone sure is acting silly," she whispered, nodding at the rest of the family talking loudly and pacing the room. "Your dad should have taken the day off and kept a lid on this," she continued with a smile. "He's quiet. That would have helped today."

Uncle Eddie was arguing with a thin woman holding a clipboard. She claimed that there was no admission order for an Edith Zelno and she could not be assigned a room. Her voice was as thin as her body and squeaked when she talked. If not for her crisp uniform, I would have thought she was a patient. A slight breeze would have knocked her down like a twig in a tornado. For a moment I thought Uncle Eddie was going to play tornado and knock her down himself. My mother had joined in the argument and it was getting pretty dicey.

"What do you think?" Aunt Edie said calmly. "Will I get in or not?"

"I'll tell you what I think," I replied. My eyebrows arched up and I leaned close to her face. "Let's let them fight it out and you and I get out of here."

Her hand flew to her mouth, stifling a giggle. I noticed her fingers were trembling. "Let's do it," she said emphatically and stood up without a moment's hesitation.

I had to jump up and head quickly for the door or lose sight of her. Without further comment she turned to her right and walked toward an exit. We soon found ourselves in a small courtyard positioned in the middle of the hospital complex.

"Doesn't the fresh grass smell nice?" she said. "I love it when it's just been cut." She moved over to a wrought iron bench and sat gingerly on the edge of its seat. She was breathing hard from the brief walk and I noticed she was perspiring heavily.

"You're pretty sick aren't you, Aunt Edie?" I asked. My chest hurt from sorrow.

She took my hand and squeezed a bit. "I'm afraid I'm very sick Billy," she said. "Maybe the doctors can help me. That's why I'm here." She smiled but I thought she sounded doubtful.

"Why don't we just go home and I'll get back to weeding your flower beds," I insisted. "I'll stick with it until the job's done." I moved away from her, gesturing for her to follow me.

"I wish life were always that easy, Billy. Sometimes there are things we don't want to face that are just not a matter or choice. This is one of them I'm afraid that I have to deal with, so I guess you'll have to work on those beds by yourself. At least for a while," she finished with a smile. "Just have them done when I get home." She winked and her hand flew to her distended stomach.

"You know Rick and I won't do it without you staying after us." I was whining and knew this was sounding like a three-year-old. "I need you to be at home, Aunt Edie." I started to cry. "Please, just go home."

She stood and held her arms out to me. I ran to her and collapsed into her, sobbing uncontrollably. I felt her shaking as she returned my tears with her own. We didn't move for a very long time, each of us letting fear and grief pour out of our hearts. The world paused for a bit and let us expel our feelings.

We finally dried our eyes and regained what little composure was possible, smiling in embarrassment at one another. "Are you ready to go back now?" she asked.

"I'm ready," I replied. For heaven's sake, she had been comforting me instead of the other way around. Even though I was not surprised, I was ashamed. I took her hand and we moved slowly towards the admitting room.

Bedlam had broken out between my mother, Uncle Eddie, and the skinny admissions clerk. They were all screaming at one another and had not even noticed that we had been gone. Rick had left too; we found him later in a doctor's lounge watching television. I asked him why they didn't throw him out, and he said they were all asleep and didn't even know he was there

Aunt Edie moved slowly up to the screaming trio and calmly raised her hand. Silence immediately fell on the room. They all turned to her, and she slowly dropped her arm, turning full attention to the admitting clerk. "Listen you little two—bit moron," she rumbled in a low voice. "You have exactly five minutes. If I am not assigned to a bed in that length of time, I will collapse right here on the floor. As a result of my fall, I will sue this hospital for five million dollars. The hospital will offer me one million dollars or I will accept no cash if they will in turn fire you." Her voice raised slightly as she said, "Now move your toothpick behind and get me a room." She stepped back and spread her arms wide, making sure there was plenty of space to fall.

"Yes, Ma'am," the clerk said, looking even thinner as she turned a sickly white. "I'll do it now." She scurried from the room before one more word could be said.

Uncle Eddie and Mother stood slack jawed. I put my hand over my mouth to conceal my smile of admiration. Aunt Edie moved shakily to the plastic couch and sat down. She wiped the back of her hand across her forehead, glanced my way, and winked.

Precisely two minutes and twenty seven seconds later my dear, feisty little aunt was in a wheelchair and heading for a private room. She proudly noted later that she was never charged a premium for having a private room. Her dignity intact, I knew she would accept any challenge this hospital had to give.

It took only moments for my mother to put the few items that her sister had chosen to bring into an aged dresser. Several changes of undergarments, a pair of slippers, three nightgowns, and two robes slid from sight in seconds. Another nightgown, slippers, and robe were laid out on the hospital bed. There would be no open-back hospital gown for her. Uncle Eddie had insisted on all of the extra changes because he felt so helpless and wanted to do something helpful out of that necessity.

The room was like a scene from the movie *THX*, where the futuristic prisoner was kept in a pure white, sterile atmosphere. The only thing in that room that wasn't white was a little plastic, curved bowl that Rick whispered was a "puke bowl". Every time my eyes drifted to this bright blue accessory my stomach turned over.

I marveled at all of the white. The bed was painted white to match the dull tile floor and walls. The mandatory hospital couch was a dull white, probably because it was yellowing with age. I resolved to get some wild flowers from our five acre woods that very day to help color this place up a bit.

"Everyone out," my mother demanded, waving her arms in an outstretched half circle, like chasing runaway chickens. "Edith has to change and doesn't need an audience." She arched her eyebrows to punctuate her comment, and we all hustled out of the sterile room.

The skinny admissions clerk came by to check on everything, nervously looking at each of us, her eyes begging for approval. Uncle Eddie was willing to give her a break, but when the *THX* room door opened, Aunt Edie saw the clerk and burst into the hall.

"Is there another problem?" she snapped.

"No, oh no, Ma'am," the clerk hastened, her skinny neck jerking back and forth in the negative. "I just wanted to make sure that you were settled, Mrs. Zelno."

I saw the twinkle in Aunt Edie's eyes. She was enjoying herself. "Very well, that will be all." She did a military about face and marched back into her room.

"Well, you folks come down and see me if you need anything." She said with a sick smile. She was backing away toward the elevator in an attempt to escape.

I lost immediate interest in her and went back into the room. Aunt Edie was sitting on the edge of the bed. She was very pale and shaky. Her little display of power took all that she possessed. She swung her feet up onto the bed, wincing in pain from the movement. Her upper body fell back with a soft thud, like a heavy package tossed a bit too rough. My mother quickly covered her bare legs to wrap the nakedness caused by the gown shifting upward. Aunt Edie weakly waved her hand up, motioning to have the bed raised. Mother knew what she meant immediately and pressed the button to raise her head.

"Billy, would you leave the room for a minute," she hoarsely whispered. "I'm afraid I'm going to get sick." She pressed her fingertips to pale lips and winced as I scuttled toward the door. Mother snatched the curved, flimsy plastic blue bowl and prepared to utilize it exactly as my brother had indicated. I could hear Aunt Edie getting violently ill as I left the room. My mother was talking softly and soothingly to her in an attempt to comfort her sister.

"Is everything all right?" Uncle Eddie asked me nervously as I pulled the door closed.

"Yeah, she's fine," I lied, forcing a smile. He didn't look ready to handle anything else right now. "Mom is helping her. Just give them a few minutes."

Uncle Eddie moved toward the closed door, hesitated, and then moved a few steps down the hall. He looked terribly old and beaten. He was a small man, barely over five foot tall, but very powerful. Today he looked shrunken, unable to cope any longer with the pressures of the world.

He turned back again for the door of Aunt Edie's room, and pushed it gently open with a trembling hand. He glanced back at me and our eyes locked. He winked a teary eye and turned away. He straightened his shoulders and stepped inside the room, softly closing the door.

Chapter 9

The great thing about being a kid is you're easily distracted. Mother wanted to stay at the hospital a bit longer, so she took me to Schoonover's pool. The Schoonovers practically owned the city of Lima in the early 1900's. They had so much wealth and power, the only thing left to do was create a legacy, man's attempt to cheat death by plastering his name in concrete for the world to see forever. Thus, old man Schoonover donated five acres of prime inner city slum land and built a huge public swimming pool. For twenty five cents each day parents could get rid of the kids and the kids beat the summer's heat.

Country kids didn't get to the pool often, so it was a treat I never passed up. Rick usually went along to stare at the high school girls who were hired as lifeguards, but he refused to ever go into the water. He claimed there was more urine in the pool than water. Signs were posted in the changing room stating "Use The Stool Not The Pool," and some smart alec had taped up a crayoned cardboard sign declaring "I won't pee in your bathtub if you don't pee in my swimming pool." It was signed Old Man Schoonover.

I don't know how much urine went in that pool,

but I do know no one went into the rest rooms
until they were ready to change and go home. That
means most of those kids either had bladders the
size of cattle troughs or they urinated into the pool.

At least half of the kids in North America were
in the pool that day. Every missing kid in a five
state area statistically had to be there. One small,
round circle of water remained unoccupied, and it
rested directly below the fifteen foot high diving
board. Whoever took the plunge had to be a really
good aim or a wet, pulpy thud would be heard as
two heads met.

No one was really swimming because there was
no room. A sea of heads like hundreds of fish co-
rks bobbed in the water. Near disasters were common at the pool. One girl dove under the water to
move to another open spot that had appeared in
the crowded pool, and before she could surface,
the spot closed. When she tried to come up for air
there was no space for her to break the surface.
Her mother saw an ankle rise to the surface, and
only a mother would instantly recognize her child's
foot. She grabbed and pulled, tearing her from the
pool like a power lifter jerking a barbell from the
floor. The girl flew upward, a cork exploding from
a bottle, and ended up above her mother's head,
balancing triumphantly on her raised arms. After
the excitement was over it was discovered that the
heroic mother had sprained her back and ended
up confined to her bed for a week.

I only saw one way into the pool that day, and
that was off the high dive into that small remaining spot. If there were any occupancy safety lev-
els, they were ignored. That small circle under the
diving board was quite simply the only access to
the water. There was no one climbing the cool
aluminum ladder that led to the springy board at

the top so I scrambled up. Looking down at the sea of people, vertigo threatened to drive me to my knees. I focused on the small blue spot in the water and quickly walked off the edge of the diving board.

The pretty high school lifeguard looked up from her entourage of pubescent male admirers just as I dropped like a bowling ball from an overpass. "Hey," she yelled, much too late for me to stop. Her mouth gaped open, perfect white teeth showing the result of a thousand dollars of orthodontics, and watched my descent. The boys never took their admiring eyes from her, thinking nothing in the world could be more interesting than the curves of her swimming suit.

If a bull's eye had been painted on the surface of that water, I could not have been more on target. I hit the small open area first, my sleek entry shooting me to the green painted concrete bottom of the pool. When I felt the rough surface of the chlorine pitted floor I pushed hard with my legs and rose, like cream in milk, to the top.

Everyone was screaming and yelling at the same time. The lifeguard was jumping up and down, much to the delight of her entourage of admirers, and blowing her official whistle. A large group of kids, both in and out of the pool, saw what I did and were cheering their heads off. I was an instant celebrity.

Screaming as loud as she could and alternately blowing her whistle, the lifeguard was trying to get me out of the pool. Capital punishment was banned for swimming pool violations, probably some time after the death of Judge Roy Bean, so I expected I would end up with the world's record for time out of the pool. I was working my way through the crowded pool, accepting the admiring comments as I struggled by with the grace of a hero athlete. I don't think I could have ever gotten to the edge of the pool if I wasn't a celebrity, but my fame gave me the privilege of people making way for me as I moved along.

Suddenly, the lifeguard had totally forgotten me. She was running towards the diving board ladder, blowing her whistle at a steady stream of would be daredevils heading up the path of fame. Normally, no one ever thought about trying to dive into a packed swimming pool, you would have to be crazy, but it now appeared that besides being an idiot, I was a trend setter. The allure of fame was just too much for these brave, stupid souls to resist. The first four boys ignored the shrieking whistle and dropped, one after the other, like bombs from an airplane.

Fortunately the whistle had made some kids react and many were leaving the water, oblivious to the real action that was going, guiltily presuming that somehow the lifeguard knew that they had just peed in the pool. Whatever the reason, plenty of room opened up for the boys to crash into the water instead of people. Finally, one fellow on the ladder stopped, and along with his hesitation the rebellious attitude drained to the bottom of the aluminum ladder. One by one the boys climbed down, beaten soldiers in the macho war of life.

I simply moved with the crowd out of the water, mingling like a terrorist escaping through the panic after a bombing. The lifeguard had her hands full with the other criminals that she had apprehended and forgot me completely. Actually, I was disappointed as well as relieved, because it was fun being a minor celebrity at the pool, but with my anonymity my stunt was promptly forgotten.

The pool began filling with people again when

the excitement was over. The copy cats from the diving board were forced to sit near the lifeguard's chair where she could keep an eye on them. The boys just assimilated themselves into the other oglers and enjoyed the afternoon lusting after their captor.

After my excitement I was pretty bored and didn't find much interest in getting back into a packed swimming pool. I wandered around the perimeter of the pool, hoping to find a group of guys I could join up with to amuse myself for the rest of the day. Schoonover pool was surrounded by a chain link fence, and the interior was a pretty large area, more or less like a prison exercise yard. About an acre of grass surrounded the cement and gave the non-swimmers plenty of space to play, picnic, and of course, look for mischief. It was mischief that I was looking for, and of course, without too much trouble, I found it.

A small group of boys whispered conspiratorially around a picnic table speckled with white pigeon droppings. The thing that attracted me to them was the boy who seemed to be their leader. This kid was perhaps as grotesque as anyone I had ever seen. He wore blue jeans cut off just above the knees, serving as a swim suit. He must have weighed around three hundred pounds soaking wet, and he wore no shirt. Fold after fold of stomach hung like inner tubes over the hidden top of his shorts. The sun had burned his blemish-covered shoulders to a lustrous pink, making him look like a huge pimpled lobster. His face was swollen with excess weight and boil-like pimples, which seemed to make his eyes almost disappear in embarrassment. Crooked yellow teeth jutted from his mouth in a perpetual buck-toothed grin, but I noticed there was no humor in his slitted eyes.

He saw me move quickly near the picnic table and pointed a sausage-sized finger at me for invading their space. "Who are you?" he rumbled in an unbelievably low voice for a thirteen-or four-teen-year-old kid. The tricep on his extended arm hung flaccidly as he pointed.

"I'm....I'm Jim," I faltered as for some reason something told me not to use my real name.

"Hey!" The grin spread, showing some gaps in the yellowed teeth further back in his mouth. "That's my name, too."

Oooookay I thought. "Wow, neat," is what I actually said.

"Come on over and sit down." Jim nodded toward the only empty spot at the picnic bench, the area most decorated by bird droppings.

"Wait a minute," one of the boys said, a fellow who was the direct opposite of the leader. He was so skinny I could see his heart thumping against his paper thin skin. "How do we know we can trust him?" he asked the group in general. He raised his eyebrows, which in turn wrinkled his forehead. He looked like an old man.

"We can trust him because he will help," the fat boy simply stated. There the discussion of my addition to the group ended.

"So what are we doing?" I asked, setting the hook that was nestled I my mouth. That stupid little sentence made me an official part of this group of hoodlums.

"How many times..." Jim paused for emphasis, nodding his head slightly and causing a minor earthquake in the flesh around his neck, "have you heard about someone flushing a cheery bomb down a toilet?"

"Hundreds," I answered. "It's the most used story ever. The problem is, it's all just that. A story."

"Exactly," Jim roared. "That's why we have to change all of that. We're going to take a story and turn it into the truth. That's what makes legends, boys. When people talk about the cherry bomb in the toilet, they'll be talking about us. Today we'll make it real," he finished triumphantly.

We all nodded dumbly, a bunch of sheep following the one with a bell around his neck, and murmured our agreement.

These guys are nuts I said to myself. The problem was, I should have said it to them. This whole idea was insane, and here I was waiting calmly to blow up Schoonover Pool's plumbing. This caper made my dive into the crowded pool look like child's play.

"Well here it is," Jim confided. He forced his hand two knuckles deep into his shorts and pulled out a two inch red firecracker with a stiff green fuse. The boys looked at it with reverence, which pleased Jim immensely. "Who's got the matches?" he asked, simultaneously putting the powerful little firecracker back into his pocket.

The little group froze when no one answered. Each boy looked at the other with the stunned expression of seeing a Judas. Who was responsible for this? We all were guilty. We hung our heads in shame, not one boy being a regular smoker and carrying matches.

"Oh, come on now," Jim grated out. "Do you mean to tell me that we've got the greatest idea since the world began and can't put it off because nobody has a match!" he ended in a bellow. I had personally lost my shame to fascination, watching his body quiver like a pile of Jell-O.

"Wait a minute," a boy sitting near our leader inserted, "my brother smokes all the time. He'll have matches."

"Well go get them then," Jim demanded. His eyes were blazing with frustration.

"No way," the boy declared. He shook blonde curly hair in a negative motion to reinforce his position. "He's eighteen and would stop us in a heartbeat. I got to steal them from him."

"How you going to do it?" another fellow asked.

"I don't really care," Jim spat out. "Just do it."

The blonde boy fell over backward in his attempt to comply with haste. Fortunately his head hit the grass instead of the concrete walkway and he simply scrambled to his feet. "Sorry," he mumbled, embarrassed by his clumsiness. "I'll be right back." He stumbled again as he ran off on his mission.

"Oh for crying out loud," Jim moaned, "we haven't a chance." He slapped his hands flat on top of the picnic bench, sending up a small white cloud of dried bird droppings. "I come up with the ideas, I got to do everything myself," he muttered, a general surrounded by idiots.

Five minutes of silence seems like five hours when you're under the critical eye of a leader. Not one boy uttered a word. The only sound was the typical pool noises that continued nearby. Jim's labored breathing could also be heard, but I didn't know if that was because of his weight or his anger.

The blonde boy at long last came running back to us, the look of triumph on his face giving away the results of his search. He held a matchbook tightly in his fist, pride bursting out all over. "I got it," he cried. "I got it," he needlessly repeated.

Jim's eyes disappeared behind his grin. "Well now, we can count on someone can't we," he proudly declared. "Come on kid, let's have it." He held out his large hand and snapped his fingers for emphasis.

The matchbook was reverently deposited on Jim's fat hand, and he deftly slid back the protective cardboard cover to reveal....two matches. We all looked at the ad for National Truck Driving School that was painted on the inside cover. This ad could not be seen when the matchbook was full, but only the top of the truck trailer was hidden by two small matches, one of them precariously bent near the pink match head.

Jim, of course, broke the silence. "Well, this isn't much to work with," he informed us. "But," he added with confidence, "you're dealing with old Jim here. I'll make it work," he finished with bravado.

"What's the plan?" I asked, feeling the excitement of a grand adventure about to begin. I was frightened and yet thrilled by all of this.

"It's simple," Jim informed with a sly wink. "We go into the locker room one at a time. There are six of us so we'll spread out and go in at thirty second intervals. That means we'll all be in there in a total of two minutes."

For the record, I knew without a moment's calculation in my head that Jim's arithmetic was off by a minute, but I wasn't going to be the fool that told him. There were at least two other puzzled looks, but not one word was said. I've always wondered if anyone else knew or if they were as dense as Jim.

"Once we're in there," he continued, "I'll light the match and old Jim here," he laid a hand on my shoulder, "will hold the cracker. He'll drop her and Blondie," he nodded at the boy who had procured the matches, "will flush. Then we'll all run like that cops are after us. Which they soon will be," he cackled

This bit of levity sobered us, the drawstrings

of our nerves pulled a bit tighter. Jim realized his error at once and was quick to add words of encouragement. "Look men, we've got to stick together now. If anyone gets caught, we don't know anyone or anything. Remember, this is history."

I don't know about the others, but I was not comforted. Still, it was too late to back out. We moved toward the cement block building that contained lockers, a bank of four showers, five urinals, and three sit down toilets. This scene was duplicated on the other side of a block wall for the girls, except the five urinals were substituted with a fourth sit down toilet.

One by one we entered the boys' side, sneaking carefully in, subtle as a tornado in a trailer park. One fellow actually pressed his back along the wall, a commando preparing to attack a pill box. Either no one cared or anyone who noticed us thought we were playing, because we all ended up inside with not one comment from anyone.

The changing room was, of course, empty. It was late enough in the afternoon that no new swimmers were likely to arrive, and of course as my brother would attest, no one would be coming in to use the urinals. We went to a narrow stall equipped with a standard brand commercial style toilet. There was no tank attached like in the home, just a water pipe coming directly out of the wall into the back of the commode. The black plastic seat was chipped and sat at an odd angle. One of the bolts that originally held it rigidly in place was missing. Very little cleaning was done in the dingy area, and the floor around the stool was sticky.

Jim took up most of the small space, resulting in some of the boys having to settle with being near the toilet instead of in the actual stall for the historic event. The firecracker was placed gently onto my sweating palm, and our leader pulled the match with the bent head carefully from the cardboard holder. He held it up to the light, studying the match carefully. It looked, with its bent stem, like a stick man with his head bowed in prayer. Jim lay the match along the length of his thumb to add support for the fragile bent spot. He put his thumb on the small sandpaper striking board and deftly pulled down. One of the boys gasped loudly as the flame burst forth, a small scent of sulfur exploding from the igniting match. With surprising agility for his size, Jim shifted the match to his forefinger and then trapped the bottom of it again with his thumb, like a mouse with its tail caught in a trap. I held the red bomb with my thumb and middle finger, end to end, the green fuse sticking out like a frog's protruding tongue. Jim touched the small yellow flame to the fuse and a shower of sparks began to fly.

"Drop it," Jim commanded through gritted teeth and I released my grip. The cherry bomb fell into the toilet with a gentle splash, a small red fish leaping in a pond. Just as the blonde boy began to flush Jim cried out "Wait!" The fuse had gone out.

Without hesitation Jim snatched the cracker out of the swirling toilet water, barely stopping it from going on its way to the Lima sewer plant. One boy made a face as our leader stood erect, holding a wet fire cracker high in the air, toilet water cascading down his pudgy arm, but no one said as much as a word. We were all nervously sweating so badly that the place stank terribly.

"Oh wow," I breathed. "How did the fuse go out? They usually aren't affected by water."

"I don't know, but we almost blew it men." Jim shook his head in relief. "Let's dry this baby off and try again." He grabbed a handful of toilet paper and gingerly dabbed at the green stub of wick.

I looked doubtfully at the thing, remembering stories about kids getting fingers blown off from defective or shortened fuses. "It's awfully short," I said, feeling immediately that it was a lame thing to say.

"You just hold tight 'til she's fizzin' real good," Jim said with a comradely wink. "I know you're a man with guts, Jim, and we can count on you."

I wondered if I had used another fake name, would Jim have thought I was this important. Well, it was too late now, because what self-respecting kid would do any thing but smile and agree to lose part of a hand if duty called. I clenched my teeth until my jaw ached and held the powerful firecracker at the ready. Sweat stung my eyes and blurred my vision, but I dared not divert my attention for even a moment. Fortunately my hands were steady so no one could see the fear I felt.

Jim pulled the last match from the flimsy cardboard pack, the top of the eighteen wheeler's trailer now showing itself in its entirety to the world. Without hesitation he turned the match to the safety strip of sandpaper and slid it across the tip in one easy motion. The flare of the match head burst into life, leaving a small but solid flame prepared to do its intended job. He carefully brought the flame to the shortened fuse and lit the appendage. A hiss of sparks showed us that the bomb was activated and would blow in an instant.

Everyone bolted as I dropped the missile into the porcelain bowl, and then the unexpected happened. The blonde kid panicked and slapped at the flush handle as he scrambled from the stall. The water in the toilet shook slightly as the mechanism let in a small amount of water, but it did not flush.

A tremendous explosion erupted from the toilet bowl, the force blasting open the stall door which hinged automatically shut, and an enormous geyser of water flew up and out, over the walls and the ceiling. Acrid smoke billowed like a trash fire from the now empty toilet, but the fire cracker had not gone down.

My ears rang from the blast. I couldn't hear the boys yelling and scrambling for the door that led to the pool area, which proved to be fortunate for me. I ran for the exit, bursting into the sunshine like a con escaping from prison. I looked through the fence and saw adults in swim suits grabbing my fellow gang members as they poured through the door. I ran to the curb and, as fate would never permit again, my mother pulled up to take me home.

"Hi, Honey. Did you have a nice time?" she said, but what I heard was "I oney, di ou av a ni ti?" My ears rang so loud from the blast of the cherry bomb that nothing registered properly on my vibrating ear drums.

"Fine," I replied, hoping that my answer fit properly with what she had just said. She was so preoccupied with worry about Aunt Edie that I wasn't noticed again until we pulled into our driveway at home. Most of the roaring inside my head was gone, helping to calm my fears that I was permanently deaf.

The local paper had a small story on the inside of the second section about vandalism at the pool. Names of the boys were not released because of their ages, but no mention was made of an escapee or implied a manhunt. The gang was true to me to the end. Besides, even if they wanted to rat me out, all they had was my phony first name. I had dodged the old bullet. My mother did think it a bit odd though that I refused to go back to Schoonover's pool for the rest of the summer.

Chapter 10

Aunt Edie was in surgery for over ten hours. They removed several tumors, one of them the size of a large apple. My father took a rare day off work and stayed home with Rick and me. In the "good old days", children were not permitted to stay home alone until at least one of them was eighteen. A decent parent in Allen County would never have dreamed of such a terrible thing. The silly part about it was that country kids ran the fields and woods at will, swimming in ponds and reservoirs, or carrying .22 caliber rifles to shoot at groundhogs. Adult rules, like anything else, do not necessarily have to make sense.

My father was working on the farm equipment that day, catching up on repairs and simple maintenance. Rick and our cousin Joe were off doing some secret older boy thing that could not be shared with a little kid. After a few games of phantom basketball, with me being the man with the ball when the great shots were taken, I became bored.

I told my father that Daisy and I were going to Larker's Pond, a mud hole owned by a neighbor about a mile away. My father mumbled something as he wiggled a bit farther under our corn planter, and I chose to take that as permission to go. The day was hot and still, and the sun baked down from a cloudless sky. The dip in Larker's Pond sounded very inviting. If my mother had been home, she would never have allowed my excursion. The pond was pretty cruddy looking, and sometimes it stank. I could have asked to be driven to Schoonover's Pool and my father would have taken me, but for obvious reasons I figured I'd have to grow a beard as a disguise before I could go back there.

Daisy hobbled along through our wheat field behind the house, following me as I sacrificed some wheat to save a longer walk to the pond. A two-acre wood stood at the back of the field, and on the other side of that was Larker's Pond. Daisy chased squirrels and barked ineffectively as they ran up the nearest tree. I was in no great hurry, so I let her run herself out. She finally came to my side, her tail wagging happily.

"What would you have done if you'd caught one of those squirrels old girl?" I said, rubbing her behind the ears. "Let's get on to the pond, okay?" I moved slowly, letting Daisy recover. Her missing leg slowed her down a bit more each year, but I didn't want to think about that. We soon passed through the woods and there stood the pond.

The Larkers had two boys and a girl, all younger than I. Although I didn't play with then very often because they were too little, I was kind of glad to see them swimming that day. Lannie, the oldest, was swinging from a tire tied to a rope on an old, bent maple tree. His sister Janet was six and waved to me from the middle of the pond. Joey, the other brother, was lounging on the other side of the pond in the mud. Strange kid. Lannie dropped from the tire with a whoop and fell into the brown water.

"Hey, how are you guys doing," I greeted. "Okay if I have a swim?" It was really just a rhetorical question because we had an open invitation to use the pond whenever we wanted, but I liked to stick to the social graces.

"Come on in," Lannie shouted, awkwardly paddling toward shore. None of the Larker kids had ever taken a swimming lesson and my mother always said one of them would drown in that filthy mud hole some day.

I was wearing an old battered pair of jeans cut off so short that the white pocket liners hung down like surrender flags on my legs. I didn't wear underwear that day because the pond water discolored them so badly they would have been ruined. It was no wonder that my mother didn't want me in that pond. Of course, this fact also made it more appealing. With a whoop I ran to the edge and launched myself into the murky water. Daisy limped over to a patch of shade and plopped down, her muzzle planted neatly between her front paws. She watched every move from her vantage point, ears twitching with each gleeful yell and splash that came from the pond.

I think Janet had a bit of a crush on me, because she really started showing off when I came on the scene. She made sure that I was watching before every dive or jump from the tire swing, trying to look pretty as she shook water from her curls. I thought the whole thing was pretty pathetic.

Lannie took a break and went over to Daisy, who gladly accepted his friendly petting. I was tired of avoiding Janet's giggles and flirts so I went over to the patch of shade too. Daisy was in dog heaven with two of us rubbing and scratching.

"Why is Joey over there in the mud?" I asked, more to create conversation than because I really cared.

Lannie shrugged thin shoulders and smiled, showing perfect white teeth as well as his pink gums. "Joey can't swim a lick," he drawled in perfect southern fashion, which always seemed odd since Lannie had never set one foot outside of Allen County. "I 'spect he wants to beat the heat though so he lies in the mud like a pig." He laughed loudly and Daisy jumped involuntarily.

"Why don't you guys get lessons some summer?" I continued, "Then all of you could enjoy your pond even more."

"No money," he replied honestly. "Mom and Dad can't afford much in the way of extras. I heard them talkin' one night about being worried they'd lose the house. I guess that stuff is a lot more important than us kids learnin' to swim. Besides, if Joey wants to learn to swim, he can do it the same as Janet and me. We just one day jumped in and splashed around 'till we could get across the pond without drownin'. It ain't no big deal."

I wasn't sure how to respond to that. Here I was, the kid who in comparison had everything, and these poor children had to worry about having a place to live. This was too much for me to handle, and I didn't want to feel the guilt either. But Lannie Larker was an okay guy. He wasn't trying to make me feel bad, he was just stating a fact, answering a question. I made a mental note to look Lannie up the next time I was lonely. He was younger in years, but in some ways he was already an old man.

We contented ourselves with small talk and just guy stuff. A breeze blew in from the west and helped cool the day a bit. Daisy relaxed and snoozed, reveling in all of the scratching and petting she had received that morning. I think I must have fallen asleep, although to this day I am not sure. I was surely completely relaxed, that much is certain. Suddenly, I was shocked into consciousness by a screaming monster dripping with feted slime. I saw it raise its scaly arms and roar in horror and hate. The sun blinded me as it blasted over the creature's shoulder, and I shrank back in terror as Daisy began barking in alarm.

My mind cleared a bit and I realized that the monster was actually Joey Larker, screaming incoherently and dripping huge globs of mud like swamp slime from rolling around at the edge of the pond. Lannie screamed at him to shut up and talk like a normal person.

Joey started to cry, but he also spoke so that we could understand him. "It's Janet," he blubbered. "Janet's gone." He sank to his knees and covered his face with his muddy little hands.

I shot to my feet, realizing what he meant. I grabbed Joey by his muddy shoulders and gave him a shake. Brown drops flew from him like rain. "Where, Joey?" I asked, trying to sound calm. "Tell me where she went down."

"Middle," the little boy gasped. "She was right in the middle and just went down."

Larker's Pond wasn't too large to begin with, but right now it looked like an ocean. There was no sign of anyone in the brown water, not even a ripple stirred the surface. Not knowing what else to do, I ran to the edge and dove in. I gulped the biggest breath of air I could handle and dove to the bottom. When my chest burned I pushed up, breaking the surface of the water and gasping for clean, fresh air.

I was near the middle but I still had a lot of area to cover. "Did she come up?" I yelled. Lannie was at the edge of the pond, a horrified look on his face.

"No!" he shouted in return.

"Send Joey for help!" I yelled and swam again for the bottom. I moved as quickly as possible, feeling my way along and praying for a miracle. I held on until I was afraid that I would black out, then pushed to the surface again.

Lannie was crying and hugging himself in frustration. "Bill, find my sister please," he begged. Joey was gone, hopefully on his way to the Larker's house for help.

I dove again, beginning to despair at the time that had gone by. If I didn't find her soon, Janet would be dead for sure. She lay in the mud right below me, my hand touching her knee as I went to the bottom again. Touching her felt like grabbing the rubbery coldness of a corpse and I almost gasped, but I stopped with a mouthful of gritty water. For some reason that made me realize how warm the water was, even here on the bottom. My lungs were screaming, but there was no way I was going to let go of her. I finally got a grip on both of her arms, which was a challenge because they were floating suspended in water, as if attempting to prevent my rescue. I pulled hard and kicked, almost losing her again as the mud pulled relentlessly on her body, reluctant to release its captive. I saw stars and flashes behind my closed lids, and my lungs felt like they would burst into flames, but I hung onto her and continued to kick toward air.

When my head exploded through the surface I almost lost my grip. My mind screamed at me to let go and concentrate only on breathing fresh, clean air to regenerate my starving cells, but my sense of duty was stronger. If I lost my hold on Janet, she would sink to the bottom again, and I knew I did not have enough strength to pull her

up again. I knew it could be too late even now, but
I wasn't going to give up for anything. She felt like
a slippery, waterlogged tree in my arms and I kept
swallowing gulps of brown water. I was able to hold
her head out of the water, but this in turn slowed
my progress toward shore. Lannie waded out and
took his sister from me, and I finally scrambled
onto the grass.

My first order of business, whether I wanted
to or not, was to throw up, emptying my stomach
of the water I had swallowed. The taste of mud
and algae made me sick again and again. I can
still remember the taste to this day, and my stomach flips over at the thought. Lannie was screaming at his sister to breathe, and I finally turned
my attention to Janet. She looked asleep, her wet
hair stringing down her cheeks and resting gently
on the grass. She was too white, showing no natural color on her cheeks. I wondered why Lannie
didn't rouse her, but only for a moment. I scrambled on hands and knees to her side, ignoring the
Canadian thistle that jammed into the heel of my
hand. I had read about CPR and first aid to drowning victims in my scouting manuals, but I did not
have any practical experience.

I rolled Janet onto her stomach and quickly
crossed her arms under her cheek, head to one
side. Our Cub Scout leader once said to pretend
you are rubbing sun tan lotion onto the victim's
back. Press it into the skin and slide your hands
slowly down the middle of the back. When I ap-
plied this technique, to my surprise water drained
out of Janet Larker's mouth. I pressed again, and
out came more water. Three and then four times I
pushed on her back. Then, I remembered to lift
her by the elbows, forcing air into her lungs.

She coughed, coughed again, and then took a

shuddering, liquid breath that imitated a victim of emphysema. I was by then lying on the ground, my face inches from hers, willing her eyes to open. I could see her eyes flying back and forth behind the closed lids, like a dreamer experiencing REM at night. Suddenly, her eyes flew open, looking into mine with confusion. "What happened?" she whispered, her eyebrows wrinkling inward.

I set up, relieved but anxious. I was trembling as the magnitude of the whole thing began to sink into my mind. Janet scrambled to her knees in alarm at the sudden roar of a Bath Township rescue vehicle, bouncing and rolling over the uneven ground as it hustled back to the pond. Lannie was jumping up and down in glee and relief. Daisy, of course, was out of control with all of this action, barking wildly and trying, in her own way, to join in the fun.

"What happened?" Janet repeated, beginning to be frightened.

"Billy Keller saved you!" Lannie shouted. "He dove right in that pond and pulled you out of there." He gestured wildly. "Then he pumped you like he was priming an old well," his arms went up and down like a pump handle, "and water came out your nose and mouth like, like, well, water!" he exploded.

Two volunteer firemen were, by this time, taking this all in. They grinned broadly and nodded their heads in approval. One of the men turned to calm an out-of-breath Mrs. Larker as she came running down the fence line from her house. I was suddenly a hero, whether I wanted to be or not.

When everyone calmed down, Janet came over to me and kissed my cheek. "I love you, Billy. You saved my life and I will never marry anybody but you. Just remember," she added solemnly, "I'll never marry anyone but you."

I beat a hasty retreat, embarrassed more by the chuckles of the rescue workers than Janet's expression of love. I wasn't going to tell anyone at home, but by the time I got there, Mrs. Larker had called my father to tell him what a hero I was. When my mother found out she went from being angry that I went swimming in that filthy pond to happy that I was there to save a life. My father just smiled, shook his head up and down, and ruffled my hair. That was the best praise of all.

Daisy was exhausted by the whole ordeal and spent the next two days sleeping on the cool cement of the garage floor. I would have worried about her except the food kept disappearing from her bowl. If she could eat, she was fine. I was worried about Janet chasing me for the rest of my life, but the next time she mentioned her outburst of love was when she laughed about the memory of that day. We talked about it at her wedding to Sam Walker, which I attended fifteen years later.

Chapter 11

Animals usually like me. We had a coop of chickens for eggs and, of course, occasionally Sunday dinner. Chickens can be pretty particular creatures, especially when you take their eggs. I was the only one who could reach under a nesting chicken and not get pecked. I would set in the penned area and the chickens would hop onto my lap to be petted. I know this is pretty weird, but both the chickens and I enjoyed this.

My favorite of the barnyard was our rooster, J.B. He was a grand old bird and was proud of being a man of the chicken coop. Each morning he flew to the top of the fence surrounding the hens and crowed at the top of his rooster lungs. If my brother or I yelled out of our bedroom window at him, he would crow again. My father didn't appreciate a crowing rooster and two boys yelling "Way to go J.B., way to go!" on a Saturday morning at dawn.

We clipped the feathers on each chicken's wings to prevent them from flying over the fence and escaping to near certain death on Bluelick Road, or becoming a snack for a neighbor's dog. J.B. was the exception because I insisted he be as free as he wanted. The thing is, J.B. didn't want to go anywhere else. For goodness' sake, he was the only male surrounded by fifty subservient females. What more could he have wanted? He still showed that he could do it, however by flying to the top of the fence each morning to crow. Just a hop to the ground and away he could go. No question about that. When he was convinced that all of the hens noticed him, J.B. would jump back down inside the fence and walk into the middle of the chicken lot. My, could that rooster strut. He was as proud and arrogant as any creature I have ever seen.

Because he was the ruler of the hen house, J.B. objected to anyone coming in and taking eggs. He would stalk around like a boxer in the ring, looking for the right opening. He waited until the offender, usually my mother, had her back turned and then ran in and pecked her ankle. He then beat his wings against her calves in an attempt to drive her from the kingdom. This did no particular harm, but it did hurt a bit and was startling. I was the only member of the family who could go anywhere in the hen house and remain unmolested. J.B. and I held a mutual respect for each other. I think J.B. knew I thought he was the coolest thing since ice and, because I had the good sense to realize it, he decided to tolerate me.

Rick entered J.B. in the Allen County fair once when he was a member of 4H. I don't think I really need to say which rooster came home with a blue ribbon for best of show. I don't know if J.B. didn't care about stupid human awards or was angry that he was away from his cackling harem for a week, but he ignored all praise and love for capturing the award. He just pecked Rick when he took him from the cage at home, wiggled free, ran to the house fence, flew to the top, crowed loudly, and jumped inside. The hens went mad, squawking and flapping their clipped wings. J.B. strutted about, glancing at each hen with chauvinistic contempt.

"Wow," I whispered, shaking my head in awe, "isn't that great."

"What do you mean, great?" my mother snapped, and stalked into the house.

I glanced at my father, who looked over, smiled, and winked, and followed after his hen.

Life was good for the old rooster, and he could have spent many years running the lives of all those hens, but one fateful day J.B. made a fatal error. He attacked my father. Now I'm not talking about a slight indiscretion here. I'm talking about a major blunder. He pecked so hard he drew blood, and there were scratches and cuts, and of course some major league screaming.

I was asked to go to the woods and pick a bouquet of wild flowers for the dining room table. I was glad to get away from the excitement anyway, so off I went. It was another warm day and Daisy tagged along, making the going pretty slow. I waited while the dog chased squirrels up the trees, then went about my work of gathering the pretty delicate flowers. I soon had a fistful and Daisy and I walked through the same path that we had created in the wheat field, not wanting to harm any other delicate stalks.

We returned to a quiet home, my mother and father were both in excellent humor and praising me for the beautiful bouquet of flowers. Somewhat confused, I went outside to play a few games of one on one basketball until dinner. After destroying three imaginary teams, I was famished.

"What's for dinner?" I called out as I walked into a kitchen full of delicious aroma.

"Corn on the cob, green beans, fresh biscuits,

and fried chicken," my mother said with pride. "And you're just in time. Get your hands and face washed and we'll eat." She rubbed my hair and turned back to the stove.

"I could eat half the world," my father declared, rubbing his hands in eager anticipation as he headed for the dining room table. "Hurry up, son, let's get the old feed bag on." He grinned and punched my arm playfully.

Maybe I would never have thought twice about what was going on if it hadn't been for my brother. Remember the look Sylvester the cat always has on his face when Granny asks the whereabouts of the Tweety bird? The cat has the bird in his mouth and just shrugs. Well, Rick was just as obvious as Sylvester. Everyone was just sitting there, smiling at me, trying to act normal.

"I'll be back in a minute," I declared, and ran out the kitchen door before anyone could object.

The chickens seemed perfectly content and normal. There was no excitement, no worry. I opened the gate and walked slowly into the chicken yard, feeling the friendly hens brush against my legs as they came to greet me. After walking completely around the chicken coop I went inside, looking at the nests with hens calmly waiting to lay an egg. J.B. was nowhere in sight.

When I confronted the merry diners, no one had moved and not a bite was taken. "I'm not hungry," I announced and went to my room. I wasn't called back to the table, and J.B. was never mentioned again.

Actually, I didn't really object to the old rooster becoming dinner. That's the way it is on a farm. Animals become like pets, but someday they are going to be eaten. I just didn't want to be part of eating J.B. This one time I didn't want to participate. Instead of making a big issue of the matter, we all just dropped the subject. Sometimes though, if I wake up early and see the sun begin to rise, I can still hear a proud rooster crow. Occasionally I whisper, "Way to go J.B., way to go," and I think I can hear him crowing again.

Chapter 12

Aunt Edie was faced with a long battle to recover from surgery. A lot had been removed, and she joked that her body looked like a network of railroad tracks. Fate being the nasty thing that it is, chose this time to transfer Uncle Eddie to Michigan with his job. Employers were demanding then as jobs were difficult to find and they didn't really care about personal problems. The only sensible solution was to invite Aunt Edie to convalesce with us.

Keller Memorial Hospital sprang into life overnight. We had a hospital bed, oxygen tanks, endless bottles of disinfectant, and new medical journals. There were more ways to get well at our house than in most third world countries.

"Is there anything else you need?" Uncle Eddie asked my mother. He was feeling guilty about leaving his wife while he went to Michigan, and his continence was showing in his eyes. Because he felt so helpless, he was throwing the only brick he had in the arsenal, money.

"Eddie," my mother assured, using her best soothing tone of voice, "there is nothing more you can do. If you lose your job there is no insurance and then the two of you won't have anything when

Edie gets well." She patted his arm for emphasis. "I'll take good care of her for you."

He swallowed hard and shielded his eyes with a trembling hand. When he spoke his voice was strained and he kept pausing between words. "I know you will, Mazie." He used my mother's childhood nickname. I don't know what it means or how she got it, but it was used as a term of endearment. "She wants to be near you until...until..."

"No." Her voice was stern now, almost demanding. "Don't you say it, Eddie. She will stay with us until she recovers from the surgery, then she can move to Detroit and live with you until she is at least a hundred."

"Yes. Yes, of course," he choked, and pulled a large white handkerchief from his back pocket, snapping it open like a magician. He covered his face and then blew his nose loudly, and I stupidly wondered if his face would wipe away when he removed the magic cloth.

"Excuse me for a moment," my mother said as she moved quickly from the room. She went to the back of the house and closed the bathroom door.

I had observed this exchange from the kitchen, sitting quietly on a tall stool that accented a counter separating our kitchen from the L-shaped dining and living room. When he was alone, Uncle Eddie shifted his attention to his surroundings. His eyes stopped at me, peering over the handkerchief like a bandit robbing a stagecoach. He lowered the white cloth, rubbing his nose and mouth as he went, and I again stupidly noted to myself that his face was still intact.

"Hey, Sport," he said with a moist, crooked smile. "Come on in here." He waved an arm and turned to a large wing backed chair near the fireplace. He sank into the chair with a tired sigh, and looked up at me again. "Come on, come on. I want to talk to you."

I of course wasn't afraid of him in the least, he was my dear uncle, the man who was a sucker for hungry boys and would spare no time or expense if Rick or I ever asked for something to eat. Yet, I did not want to go near him, for a reason I could not explain. "I was just going outside," I answered lamely, not moving from my stool.

"You can go outside later," he said, waving at me again. "Come over here for a minute. I want to talk to you."

Reluctantly I slid from the stool, my hands flat and palms down, squeaking slightly as they dragged over the countertop. I walked to the edge of the dining room table and stopped. "What do you want?" I asked hopefully not sounding too suspicious.

"I want to talk to you about something very serious and I want you to be closer when I speak. Now please come here," he repeated.

I moved slowly to the front of the chair, looking down at his sad face. He motioned to the floor with a thick index finger. "Sit. Sit right on the floor in front of me for a minute. You're young, you don't need a chair for just a bit."

I sank to the floor, crossing my ankles Indian style, and rested my forearms on my knees. I looked up at him and waited for him to begin. "Your Aunt Edie is very sick," he began. "She has cancer." He paused and drew a deep breath. "The doctor cut a lot of it out but he couldn't remove all of it. Do you understand?"

I nodded, but I didn't really totally understand. Why didn't they cut all of the cancer out?

As if he had heard my thoughts, Uncle Eddie continued, "Some of the cancer is in areas of her body where it can't be cut out, because it would kill her."

"But won't she die if they leave the cancer in?" I interjected.

"Maybe, but she would die for sure if they cut out any more, so we have to get some strong medicine and try to kill just the cancer that's left."

My head was reeling and I wasn't sure if I even wanted to have this conversation. However, since we were, I had no choice but to forge ahead. "So, is Aunt Edie going to die or not?"

"No," he almost shouted, and I flinched. "I mean, no" he repeated, softly this time, "at least we hope not. But," almost like an afterthought, "that could happen, Billy. That could happen." He looked as if he had just realized that as a possibility.

"I don't want her to die," I stated the obvious.

"None of us want that, Billy." He smiled at me and I wondered why he looked so bleary, until I realized my eyes were full of tears.

"Well, it's just not going to happen," I declared and jumped to my feet. I turned and almost ran into my red-eyed mother, who had come back into the room. "It's not going to happen, do you hear me?" I yelled at her and ran from the house

I cried for a long time, just sitting in the dark coolness of our barn on the dirt floor and scratching Daisy's ears. Summer was a time for fun and good times, it was not intended to be a time to worry about someone you loved. Finally, I made a decision. Aunt Edie would not die because I wasn't going to allow that to happen. That fact made me feel much better, and I went about my summer with a renewed confidence.

I asked to visit the hospital after about a week. My mother told me that visitors were, at this point, welcome and we could visit that very morning and then eat lunch at the Kewpee. She made me dress up like I was going to a wedding or church on Sunday, which I objected to, of course to no avail.

We entered the sterile building with the awful antiseptic smell and took the elevator to the fifth floor, which was used as the recovery area after major surgery. I was in pretty good humor as we walked down the hallway. As I turned into her room at a fairly smart pace, I slammed face first into Doc Hacook's huge belly and bounced, like a gymnast on a trampoline, backwards and to the ground.

"Well, what have we here?" Doc wheezed, hands resting on broad hips and looking down at my surprised form sprawled on the floor.

"Wow," was all I could say, shock and a little bit of fear blocking out any other comment.

Doc reached down and circled my arm with sausage sized fingers. He effortlessly stood erect, pulling me to my feet as easily as if he were picking up a piece of paper dropped on the floor. "You need to be a bit more cautious, young fellow," he said, jerking a thumb inside the room. "If that would have been our patient here you ran into, we would be sewing her stitches up again."

"Sorry, Doc," I apologized, really feeling bad that I could have hurt Aunt Edie.

"Say, have you been regular?" He moved to the dreaded subject so quickly it was as if the other incident had not happened. "I forgot now. Did we soap you up or did you go on your own?" he asked with a mischievous twinkle in his eye.

"No, no, sir," I hurried, my heart suddenly pounding. "I got straightened out on my own, and I've been fine ever since."

"Harrumph!" He seemed disappointed. "Well, I

guess you were just being stubborn then, eh?"

"Yes, sir," I lied. "Just stubborn."

"Well then, get in there and see your aunt," he demanded. "Hello, Waneta," he added to my mother. "She's going a bit stir crazy and wants some company."

"What do you think, Doc?" Mother asked softly.

"Well, we can't tell," he said too loudly. "Let's wait for the radiation treatments and see how they work." He patted her shoulder and moved down the hall. "Give it time, Waneta," he said as a final comment.

"Give what time?" came a small voice from the hospital room.

We hurried in to see Aunt Edie, looking pale and tired, sitting in her bed, legs bent and back somewhat straight, looking like a swimmer poised on the starting blocks. She looked almost funny, so I smiled.

"Weird looking, isn't it?" she said. "This is the only position I can find that doesn't hurt. But, at least I can stop the hurt." She winked at me and tried to smile, the pain showing in her eyes despite her best efforts.

"Doc Hacook said you'll be doing better in time," my mother said. "He said you just need rest."

"That I do," she agreed. " I feel like I've been in a war and my side lost." She winced and shifted in the bed. "I sure could have done without all of this."

She looked absolutely terrible. Her hair was very fine and was plastered down on her head in some places and stuck out in others. A large sore rested at each corner of her mouth and the absence of makeup made her look even more pale and ill. Her hands trembled so much that the plastic intravenous lines running into her arms rattled slightly against the metal pole holding strange

colored bags of liquid. The room smelled of antiseptic, healing flesh, body waste, and pain. Yes, I
truly believed I could smell her pain.

"We've got your bed ready in the living room,"
my mother said. "Dr. Fleckner told us what we
needed and the place looks like a Red Cross center,"
she added with a smile.

Dr. Fleckner was a cancer surgeon who was
known as the best in Lima. He was big as a wres-
tler, with hands so huge it was amazing he could
perform delicate work. He walked with a pro-
nounced limp because one leg was a prosthesis.
The story that was told regarding the loss of his
leg was that, as a boy, he was injured in an accident. The doctor who treated him tried to repair
the badly injured limb and basically botched the
job. Another surgeon ultimately had to remove the
leg. The boy's life long dream from that moment
was to become a surgeon with enough skill to save
people from unnecessary suffering. Somewhere
along the way he turned to cancer as a specialty
and truly was the best in his field. He was known
as a man of great compassion and took very personally the outcome of his patients.

"Well, I don't want to be a bother," Aunt Edie
was saying. "I've always said if you're going to be a
burden on someone then you shouldn't be there."

"You can't be a burden to me," my mother answered softly, "I'm only burdened when you're not
with me."

I decided to get out of the room for a while at
this point, having the good sense to let these two
sisters share some time together. Of course, when
you're hanging around a hospital there is not a
whole lot to do, so I wandered the floor, looking
into each room as I passed. Most were occupied
by sleeping people, looking drugged and miser-

able. I was about half way around the large circular floor with the nurses station in the middle when I saw him. He had to be the thinnest man I have ever seen. Concentration camp thin. At first I wasn't sure that he had eyes, they were sunk so deep into their sockets. A wisp of hair at the top of his head gave him the look of a Dr. Seuss character.

"Boy, come in here." His voice was high pitched and thin, like finger nails scraping a chalk board.

I hesitated, not really fearing the man as much as I was revolted by his physical condition. Almost hypnotically, I moved into the room. He sat in a wheel chair, wearing dark blue pajamas that hung like draperies from a single pane window. I noticed as I entered the room that he wheezed when he breathed, although there was no oxygen tube hooked to his nose.

"You look like a boy that's bored," he screeched in his birdlike voice. A long skeleton hand waved at me to come closer. "I'll bet you're a smart boy, too." He smiled, looking like a Halloween pumpkin with several yellow teeth showing around black spaces in between.

Just two steps inside the doorway, I was prepared to run if necessary. He was so frail I can't believe he could have held himself up, so I had little to worry about. Horror movies flashed through my head, with monsters shooting lightening from their hands and undead creatures stalking victims. This old man certainly seemed to fit this profile, and even though in my heart I knew scary stories weren't true, when you're confronted with one in real life it is very frightening.

"Do you play checkers boy? I'll bet you're a dandy checker player aren't you?" He rubbed his bony fingers with delight, and I looked hard for fire or lightening to burst from his palms.

"I play checkers," I answered, wondering where this was going.

"Good, good. Oh, how delightfully good." The old man actually cackled. "Look over there on that dresser, my boy. Do you see that box?"

At first I thought that there was a shape that consisted of Scotch tape and masking tape. When I walked over to the small chest of drawers, I could see that resting on the top was, indeed, a box. It had been repaired again and again with tape. I was not sure that I could touch it without the ancient mass falling apart.

"That's it. Bring it here now." The old man was anxious now, seeming to fear that something would go wrong.

I carried it to him gingerly and he snatched the box with bony claws. He snatched off the top like a bear tearing into a honeycomb. Amazingly, there was no damage to the frail looking container, and the old man took out a flat piece of heavy cardboard that was folded in half. When he unfolded it I noticed that a piece of yellowed strapping tape held the board together.

"What do you think, lad?" he asked and his eyes sparkled with pleasure. It was a checker board, with an emphasis on the was. Some of the squares were worn so badly that he had drawn the boundaries with a black marker. The black squares were colored in black, the red squares were mostly worn white. One spot had a piece of masking tape covering a hole. The playing pieces were made of wood, surprisingly well preserved except for the smooth areas worn away by handling. The red discs were actually made of cherry, the black discs of walnut.

The old man noticed that I was admiring his

set and said with pride, "I carved these beauties myself. Someday I'll get to the board and carve me one, but I've been kind of weak for a time, you know?" His jack o'lantern grin spread wide. "Come, sit right here." He pointed to a vinyl-covered chair that was in front of his wheel chair. He pulled over the hospital table on rollers. It looked like a giant tongue sticking out. This separated us and enabled the checker board to be set up. "Black or red?" he demanded.

"Black," I said automatically, wondering why I had done this.

"Excellent choice, my boy," he screeched. A fit of coughing made him pause. When he was through, he actually looked better because the exertion put some color back into his cheeks. "Red is my favorite. You're very kind to let me take my choice."

"But I didn't," I began, then just shrugged. "Why don't you go first, sir."

"My Christmas." He shook his head slowly, the palms of his hands held skyward. "There's not one in a hundred boys that would show that kind of respect to an elder. Sir. Yes, it was 'sir' that you said." He placed a hand on each sallow cheek in mock surprise. "Actually, my lad, I insist that you go first."

I smiled and set up my checkers. The old man moved slowly but deliberately. When he was ready he reached into a pocket in his pajamas and laid a quarter beside the checker board.

"What's that for?" I asked.

"If you beat me, boy, the quarter is yours," the old man said solemnly.

"I don't gamble," I said with resolve. "My parents don't allow it," I added.

"Good for you! Excellent! Yes, yes good, good,

good for you my boy," he cried, like an excited child at the carnival. "I shouldn't want to corrupt a fine lad like you," a fit of coughing stopped him for a moment, "but this isn't a bet. I'm hiring you to work for me."

"Hiring me?" He had my interest.

"Absolutely, my boy. Beat me and you earn a quarter. Lose and you don't get paid."

"I guess that's not gambling," I thought aloud.

"Of course it isn't," he demanded. "Now let's get on with it."

He beat me in eight moves. The next game I did better, I lost in nine. I pretty much lost track after that, but I would guess we played close to thirty games of checkers and I never won once. I got kind of obsessed with that quarter, thinking more about it than my game, although I don't suppose it would have made any difference. This skinny old man was the Bobby Fisher of checkers. His quarter was as safe as the gold at Fort Knox.

We played for what did not seem to be a terribly long time, and during one typical match while I was being soundly defeated, the old man sighed, leaned back in his wheel chair, and closed his eyes. I thought he must be resting for a moment, but after a while realized he wasn't going to move.

"Sir. Excuse me, sir." He didn't respond. His chin almost touched his chest and his mouth hung open. A small drop of saliva gathered on his lower lip. Suddenly it hit me, the old man was dead.

Panic seized me like a lion taking down a gazelle. Was I responsible? Did I somehow kill him? Suddenly I heard a noise, which was very soft and yet persistent. How many people had the opportunity to witness the soul leaving the body? That had to be what I was hearing. I leaned forward an inch at a time, like a caterpillar moving slowly and cautiously over a leaf. My head grew light and dizzy because I was holding my breath in anticipation of this incredible event.

Then the noise grew louder. Just imperceptibly at first, finally increasing a decibel at a time. He was snoring. Suddenly the old man let out a snore that bolted me from my chair, with shock and relief flooding through me at the same time. He wasn't dead after all; I hadn't killed him. I had just worn him out.

As I turned to leave, a young woman walked into the room, her long blonde hair hanging in soft layers down the back. She wore a gray tweed suit and black high heels, giving her the look of a business professional. Her eyes had dark circles under them, showing her fatigue. "Well, hello," she said with a warm smile. "It appears that Dad captured a checkers player."

"Yes, Ma'am," I replied. "He's your father?"

"Yes he is."

"I don't even know his name. He sure is a good checkers player though," I said.

"He should be good," she said and looked fondly at her sleeping father. "His name is Stan Bledsoe and he was the national checkers champion in 1921."

"Wow. No wonder I couldn't beat him," I replied with genuine awe.

"He could play checkers every waking moment. I've tried to get him to let me replace that old set he uses but he won't part with it. I guess it's his anchor to younger days."

"What's wrong with him?" I asked. "I mean why is he in the hospital?"

She sighed and shrugged. "He's just worn out. Dad's ninety years old and his body is just tired. I don't thing I'll have him too much longer." A tear appeared from out of nowhere and rolled down her cheek.

"Well, I should be going," I said, not knowing what else to say.

"Thank you for giving Dad some of your time. He loves to play and I'm sure he would like to thank you. Are you visiting someone here in the hospital?"

"My aunt is here on this floor," I replied

"And how is she doing?" she asked politely.

"Oh, just fine," I said. "She's going to be just fine."

"Well, good. If you're up here again, come back so Dad can thank you when he's awake. And maybe even play checkers with him again," she added with a smile.

"Yes, Ma'am, I'd like that. Good-bye now." I moved into the hallway.

"Good-bye," she said, and went to sit by her father.

I went back to Aunt Edie's room and found her and my mother talking like two school girls. They really had not noticed that I had been gone. I listened to their chatter, feeling a bit like an eavesdropper, and waited for them to finish.

Chapter 13

A hot, rainy morning greeted us the day Aunt Edie left the hospital. Uncle Eddie hired a private ambulance company to bring her to our house, an extravagance that was unheard of at that time. He rode with her from the hospital, along with my mother and the paramedics. My father was the chauffeur that took them to the hospital so there would not be a car stranded in the parking lot.

Daisy was restless, probably sensing the tension that I felt, and she tried to occupy herself with our pet barn cat, Clementine. They actually got along quite well, with no typical dog versus cat hatred.

Clementine was an exercise in physiology for my benefit. My parents wanted me to learn about the birds and the bees, thinking that if they got a cat who eventually became pregnant, I could see the miracle of life firsthand. Little did they know that Rick, our cousin Joe and I found a bag of pornographic magazines in a ditch, resulting in a rather bizarre lesson of strange sex. To this day I find it amazing that some of the things are physically possible.

The cat was not cooperating, because as time went on the blessed event had never happened.

Frustrated, my parents considered getting several Tom cats in hopes of forcing the issue. As cats go, Clementine was attractive enough. She was gray with one white foot and one white eye. I know she interacted with other cats, because occasionally she would come home after a night out on the town with scratches or patches of fur missing. My brother quipped that maybe our stupid cat didn't like boys. A glare from our father stopped the remarks.

Shorty Walters, the man who delivered our fuel oil during the winter, came by at least once during the summer to do a tank inspection. He stopped that day and saw me watching the dog and cat playing together. "Hi, Shorty," I called out.

"Hi yourself, Billy," he answered with a wave. Shorty was, of course, a nickname that Roy Walters was tagged with because of his five-foot, one-inch frame. Instead of feeling resentment of this moniker, Shorty actually seemed a bit proud of the handle.

"Tank inspection?" I asked, just being conversational.

"Yeah, we don't want any accidents out here this summer." He gestured toward Daisy and Clementine, who were rolling in the grass, growling and biting playfully. "Look at that. Two friends having a friendly tussle."

"They've always gotten along," I agreed. Clementine grew tired of the game and jumped away from the dog. "Daisy gets a bit rough though."

The cat shook itself and then strolled toward us, wanting to check out our visitor. Daisy, not wanting to end the game, bounded after Clementine with a playful bark. This forced the cat into action, and she leaped in two graceful strides into the arms of Roy Walters. "Well now, that's a cat," he cried out with delight. "Is this your favorite?"

"Actually, my favorite cat we ever had was Felix," I reminisced.

"Felix," Shorty echoed. "Like the cat in the comic papers."

"Yeah. Real original wasn't it. Anyway, we went on vacation one summer and asked a neighbor to feed the cat and the chickens while we were away."

"What about the dog?" Shorty interrupted.

"Our dog had died about two months before, so we decided to wait until we got back from vacation before getting a pup."

"Very sensible," Shorty agreed. He rolled Clementine onto her back and began scratching her stomach. The cat responded by arching her back and letting her head lull in pleasure. She began to purr with gusto.

"In fact, Daisy is that very dog we got to replace Nipper."

"Nipper?"

"Yeah, the dog that died" I explained. "Well, Felix must have thought we left him for good, because he refused to eat. We never thought about checking in with the neighbor, because we knew she would take care of things."

"Very reasonable," Shorty agreed, peering oddly at Clementine as she lay spread out like road kill.

"When we got home, Felix came running or rather staggering, and cried like a baby. He went into the chicken coop for company and waited to die. That poor old cat ate like he had never had a bite of food in his life. He looked like he had been in a prison camp."

"Wow," Shorty whispered, obviously entranced by my story.

Encouraged by his enjoyment of my tale, I prepared to continue. "Then we...." I began but he interrupted.

"And what about the cat? Was he dead when you got home?" he asked, looking up from Clementine's stomach.

"What do you mean, Shorty?" I asked, feeling a bit perplexed and irritated at the same time. "I just told you that Felix was half starved and lived with the chickens until we got home, then ate like a pig. He was really skinny and weak, but he recovered just fine." I blurted this all out in one long breath, so I paused and inhaled deeply before I continued. "But I just told you all that. I guess you just weren't listening."

He was peering at Clementine and again seemed preoccupied. He looked up at me and stared for a long moment, seeming to struggle in an attempt to focus his eyes on my face. "I'm sorry, Billy." His face reddened in embarrassment. "It's just that, well, I noticed something, and it took my attention for a minute."

"What the devil are you talking about, Shorty?" I inquired, by now more curious than angry.

"Well, I noticed that old Clementine here isn't a girl."

I stared at him, dumbfounded. Farm people first of all don't make mistakes, and secondly someone would have looked. Wouldn't they? "You're telling me that cat's a boy?" I asked incredulously.

"Yep. He's a good old Tom," Shorty announced proudly. He roughed up Clementine's belly and the cat responded with a playful slap at his hand with a paw.

We stood quietly staring at each other for a very long moment, then we both started laughing. Shorty laughed so heartily that Clementine was startled and leaped from his arms, twisting in the air and landing lightly on her, I mean his, feet. I was wondering how to handle this one, but decided it was too funny not to make a big deal out of it. Shorty walked around toward our fuel oil tank, and I could hear him laughing all the way.

The day was too serious to make much out of the discovery since Aunt Edie needed so much care, but eventually Clementine's name was officially changed to Clem.

Shorty finished his inspection and went on his way, still chuckling I might add, when the ambulance pulled into our drive. It moved slowly and smoothly like a ghost floating along the surface of the ground. The flashing warning lights blinked on and off like a giant Christmas display, and I could hear the faint click click as the tube shaped flasher alternately sent and then withheld its electrical impulse. My father pulled in close behind and parked the car on the stone pathway that led to the barn. The car tires cracked on the crushed stone almost angrily, accentuated by the silence created around us.

The ambulance rear doors flew open like a rent in a piece of fabric. A man wearing a white jump suit fell from the opening and landed on his feet as gracefully as a cat. A second man in an identical jump suit more or less lumbered down to the ground. His belt was covered by a huge belly that must have begged for more beer. The driver and another attendant in the front seat of the vehicle exited and joined their fellow crew members. My mother stepped out gracefully and accepted the extended hand of the heavy man. Uncle Eddie jumped to the ground unassisted, and I thought to myself that this was beginning to look like a clown car at the circus. I expected more people to flow from the ambulance like sugar grains spilling from a box, but no one else followed.

The heavy set man was in charge, and I was

impressed with his efficiency. He gave short but precise commands which were unflinchingly followed by the other crew members. They reached inside the ambulance and pulled out a bed on wheels that contained Aunt Edie. I stood at the side of the vehicle and it looked like a tongue sticking out of a mouth. When the bed cleared the back of the ambulance, they pushed a button at each end of the bed and the wheels sprang down on accordion style struts that resembled the legs on an erector set.

Aunt Edie saw me and gave a weak wave. She winked and tried to smile, but it came out more like a grimace. She was wheeled to our back steps and then they lifted her carefully onto the back porch. I had been frozen in place, unable to react or move as the group moved about their work, but as the back door closed I was released from my fascination and sprang toward the door.

I found them in our living room, transferring her to the hospital bed that was to occupy most of her time. Despite the gentle hands of the ambulance crew, she groaned as they moved her. Uncle Eddie stood nearby, grim faced and pale. I noticed his hands were shaking. The room was cheery and bright, but the mood was so glum that nothing helped. I felt like we were in a funeral home. Everyone was whispering and talking about Aunt Edie like she wasn't there.

"I feel like a piano," she said and all eyes turned toward her bed. A faint smile played on her thin lips and her eyes were bright and twinkling.

"What?" Uncle Eddie blurted, moving close to her side.

"I said I feel like a piano," she repeated. "I was just moved in by Mayflower movers and dropped here in the living room. That's exactly what it seemed like to me."

I laughed out loud, relief flooding through me. As long as she could keep her sense of humor, my aunt would be all right. My laughter released everyone else. The tension broke and all of us started laughing, even the ambulance attendants joined in the humor. They made a quick exit and left us to get used to our new arrangement.

We all sat in the living room and just talked, because being near Aunt Edie was important to us all right at that moment. She seemed to be asleep and unaware of our presence. I noticed again that people ignore the sick person. She was discussed in the past tense, as if we were remembering the good times we had when she had come to visit. I began to feel like she was already just a memory and I didn't like that feeling at all.

"How do you folks expect a girl to get her beauty rest?" she grumbled. This arrested our attention again, and I noticed her eyes were closed. "I could sleep if you people would get out of my bedroom," she continued, smiling but still keeping her eyes closed as if she were talking in her sleep.

"Okay, Honey," Uncle Eddie said, patting her with gentleness.

"Let's go outside," my mother suggested. "We can enjoy the breeze."

"I've got to go anyway," Uncle Eddie answered. "Detroit is a long drive away." He knelt beside the bed and took her hand in his, pressing it to his lips.

"We'll wait outside," my mother repeated, gesturing at us to head for the kitchen door.

We heard him crying as we left the room.

Chapter 14

Life is necessary for existence, thus, as the old saying tells us, it goes on. We fell quickly into a routine that consisted of health care and comfort as well as normal activities that simply continue. Near the end of week two of Aunt Edie's stay with us I wanted to go fishing. My parents were anxious for life to get back to normal so they agreed to take a friend and me to Hog Creek, a narrow body of water that flowed through Allen County. I chose Bud Campbell to go with me, and still they agreed. I guess they thought I really needed a break.

Bud met us on the Cool Road bridge that carried traffic over the creek. Fishing pole and bait in one hand, a cardboard box for a tackle box in the other, and a dirty straw hat set off his look to a tee. Almost intentionally he looked like a latter day Huck Finn. He even sported a green-stemmed piece of wheat jutting from one side of his mouth.

I, too, could have walked to the creek, but my mother would not have that. It was about three miles, which to her was too far. My bicycle was out of the question because it would be too hard to transport equipment. I felt a bit embarrassed because I had a fairly new metal tackle box and a high quality Garcia fishing rod and reel combo, compared to Bud's piece of junk and his cardboard box. Bud was all smiles though and didn't seem to notice.

"Good morning, Bud," my mother said politely. She had rolled the car window down and glared at him suspiciously.

"Morning,Mrs. K," he responded, wheat stalk bouncing in his mouth as he talked.

"Do you have cigarettes with you, Bud?" Her eyes narrowed slightly to help her detect a lie, and her nostrils twitched, almost like she was trying to smell tobacco.

"No, Ma'am," he responded with a solemn shake of the head. "Cigarettes are bad for us young boys, and besides it ain't legal for us to have 'em." I could swear there really was a halo over his head.

"Uh huh," she answered, almost ready to change her mind about our little outing.

I quickly unloaded my equipment and we turned toward the embankment that led to the water. I waved to my suspicious mother and gave the grinning Bud a push away from the car.

"Billy." Her tone brought me back to the car. She looked into my eyes and stared for a long moment. I could see my reflection in her irises. "I'll check your breath when you come home," she whispered. Before I could comment she pulled her head in the window and drove away. "See you in three hours," she called out as she waved good-bye.

Bud and I half ran, half slid down the steep embankment, quickly moved along the bank of the creek, and soon we were out of sight of the bridge. We collapsed on a flat, grassy area, and Bud pulled a crumpled pack of Marlboro's from his pants pocket. He offered me one but I shook my head.

"I'll be checked for smoke breath at home," I

said reluctantly. "I'd better not."

Bud grinned and gave me a wink. He shoved his hand in his pocket and pulled out a pack of Black Jack chewing gum. I grinned back at him and took a Marlboro. We smoked leisurely and not a word was spoken. The water was calm and a gentle breeze shook the leaves in nearby trees. I watched clouds floating high in the sky, their changing shapes making me dizzy.

"You want to fish?" Bud asked.

"I don't know. I'm kind of enjoying just loafing around right here," I replied lazily.

"You want another smoke?"

"No. You know what though? We could move down around that bend over there," I gestured toward a sharp bend about one hundred yards further downstream, "and see if we can find old Flossie's fishing hole."

Flossie Henderson lived in a run-down farm house near the bridge over Hog Creek. She claimed to know a special place where the fish schooled and were always hungry. Fishing stories were just as prevalent in our county as anywhere, but this was one time that there was proof. Flossie had dozens of pictures showing stringers of blue gill, bass, and catfish. That was enough to create the legend and make everyone look for the famous spot. One fellow claimed he hired a private detective to follow the old woman to the sacred spot. She did not fish once while the investigator watched her, but the day after the surveillance was dropped, Flossie added a new picture to her collection.

"Why do you think we could find old Flossie's spot?" Bud asked, skeptical but obviously interested.

"I just figure we've got as much a chance as anyone," I countered. "Think about it for a minute

Bud. Flossie's old, right?"

"Yeah, I can't argue that." Bud agreed.

"Well, then, do you see her going too far down the creek to fish? She's too feeble to get too far, unless she takes the tractor or something. But I doubt that, because someone would surely track her if she's out there running through brush and weeds with a piece of machinery."

"Maybe it's not a tractor. Maybe she's got a go-cart in her barn."

"Come on," I urged. "Let me show you something." Bud followed me as I climbed a steep slope until I could see the back of Flossie's house across a hay field. "That's her place. Do you see it?"

"Yeah, of course I can see it. I'm right here looking with you," Bud said, getting a bit irritated.

"No, no. I don't mean do you see her house. I mean do you see the path?" I cried.

"Shoot the bed," Bud drawled. Indeed, there was a faint but distinct pathway leading to a spot just around the bend of the creek. "Why didn't we see that before?"

"Because that hay was cut, I'd guess, maybe a couple of days ago. She's worn out a spot that didn't show because clover grows up and then bends over. It's covered the path but the bailer got pretty close to the ground. I'd guess in a day or two, especially if we get any rain, that path won't show any more. It could even be the way the sun's hitting it right this second. It may not show again, ever. Cripes, I was just going to look for a short cut to her back door. I sure never expected to find Flossie's path."

"Let's get our gear and find the end of that path," Bud exclaimed, "before it's gone."

We scrambled back to our fishing gear and ran around the bend to the creek. The ground sloped upward as we moved on and gradually became a level plane from Flossie's house to the creek. We found that by dropping to ground level we could still see the path that led straight to the edge of the water.

"This makes sense," I whispered. "She couldn't very well climb hills as old as she is"

"Yeah," Bud whispered in return. "But I do have a question."

"What?" I hissed in his ear."

"Why are we whispering?" he asked.

We instantly lost complete control and howled with laughter. I laughed until my side hurt, then lost control and howled again.

"Listen!" Bud suddenly was no longer laughing. He rolled onto his stomach and looked around, like a ground hog sticking its head up to see what was causing the disturbance.

I drifted off a few more chuckles, not realizing at first that he was serious. Then I heard it too, a noise in the underbrush not far from our vantage point.

"What is it?" Bud whispered, falling back into our secretive communication.

"I think it's..." I began, then my words froze in my throat. Rising up in a patch of raspberry bush and growling angry was a bear

"Do we run?" Bud asked, his voice squeaking in fear.

The question became a mute point as the bear came down on all fours and charged in our direction. Instantly we ran in the direction of the bridge, both of us yelling and screaming for all we were worth. The bear was roaring back at us, sounding like a bull chasing a matador.

The three of us were running with our heads down, all concentration being committed to pure speed. I suddenly realized that the bear had run past us, howling and bellowing like a scalded cat. I yelled at Bud to stop and we stumbled to an awkward halt, the bear crashing on ahead at a high rate of speed. Perhaps it would have kept running and we would have escaped, but a tree root growing in a half moon arc from out of and then back into the ground, caught the bear's front leg. He tumbled head over heels exactly two and a half times and scrambled to his feet, legs churning in the exact direction he was pointed. Because of the additional half tumble, he of course was rerouted back toward us.

Bud and I looked at each other in dismay for an instant and then did the only possible thing we could do, we ran. Common sense did not prevail here, because we ran side by side. If we would have split up, at least one of us would have been able to escape. The bear would have been forced to make a decision. Instead we ran along the water's edge like two sprinters racing for the finish line.

Suddenly, a voice rang out as clear as a siren warning. "Brutus!" it roared, and the bear and we boys slid to a halt. I smelled damp, dirty fur and realized that the bear had stopped in line with Bud and me. I looked out of the corner of my eye and saw him panting and slobbering a mere two feet from my side. Standing in front of us, all eighty-nine pounds of her, was Flossie Henderson.

She was wearing bib overalls that were at least four sizes too large, the legs rolled up to the top of her Wolverine work boots. She carried a cane fishing pole with about four feet of line and a faded balsa wood bobber. She did not have any tackle box or any visible bait. A red checkered Pendleton shirt with the sleeves rolled to the elbows and the collar buttoned around her long neck accentuated her pretty face. It was surprisingly devoid of wrinkles, and if she had been wearing makeup, would have looked even younger. A faded Cleveland Indians baseball cap hid all but thick gray bangs spilling onto her forehead. A stringer of over twenty fish was slung over her shoulder.

Completely ignoring us, the bear ambled over to her and sat back on its haunches. This move brought the beast's muzzle level with Flossie's face. They stared at each other for a few seconds and finally Flossie leaned forward and kissed the bear gently on the nose. Rumbling with pleasure, the bear licked her cheek in return.

"Oh for sh...I mean, oh shoot," Bud gasped.

"Hello, boys," Flossie said sweetly, smiling at us as she brought the stringer off her shoulder. The bear smacked his lips in anticipation. "Brutus wouldn't hurt you. He saw your fishing poles and figured you might have fish. That's all he really wanted." She scratched the bear's ears before removing a large pan fish from the stringer and holding it out to the bear. The fish slid from sight into the large mouth in an instant.

My heart was pounding so hard I could hardly hear what she said. I blinked in disbelief at the sight of this bear and this old woman. I wasn't sure if I wanted to laugh or cry. "This your bear?" I asked. What a brilliant question.

"No, honey, this bear doesn't belong to anyone except of course God. He's just a neighbor of mine that hangs around and likes to eat fish." She deftly removed another fish from the stringer and fed it to the hungry animal. "He probably don't like anybody any better than I do, but feed him fish and he thinks you're all right."

The bear whined, which was more of a growl,

and she reached for yet another fish, this time a large catfish. Before serving it to the bruin Flossie pulled a hunting knife from her belt and sliced off the hard, thorn like spine sticking out of the top of the fish. She smiled fondly as Brutus held the fish in his huge paws while his powerful jaws did their work.

"Bears can't get bottom feeders," Flossie said. "You have to cut the hard spine off the cat or it will stick in the roof of his mouth. I'm sure that would be very painful for Brutus, and I don't think I want to be too near him if he's in pain." She turned her attention back to her furry friend and held his cheeks in her small hands. "Isn't that right, sweet-heart." She gave a playful tug at his face and Brutus responded, after licking a few remaining bits of fish from his lips, by nuzzling Flossie's neck.

"Well, I guess we're not going to die," Bud gulped. "Course, I think I need to change my un-derwear." He looked doubtfully at the front of his jeans.

"Honey," Flossie said with a laugh, "You're not going to die today, at least by this bear." She fed another fish to Brutus before continuing. "What are you boys doing today? Let me guess," She went on without pause, "you're looking for old Flossie's fishing hole."

"Well, I guess that's the truth," I admitted, a bit embarrassed by the revelation. "Everyone I know wonders where it might be," I added with a smile.

"And well they should," she almost shouted in triumph. "You can see for yourselves that there are plenty of fish, at least in one spot along this old creek."

"I don't suppose you'd tell us where your spot is?" Bud asked hopefully.

Flossie laughed a soft, yet robust sound of someone who enjoyed the humor of life. "Now, boys, if I told, the mystery would be over, everyone would fish out of my spot, and old Brutus here would go hungry." Yet another fish was gobbled by the bear.

"We wouldn't tell no one," Bud promised. "We'll swear a death oath on it, won't we Bill?" He looked at me for reinforcement.

"Yes. Yes, we sure will." I tried to sound convincing. "Not one word to anybody."

"You boys are too much," Flossie giggled. "I'll tell you what. I'll show you right where to fish. What do you think of that?"

We must have looked ridiculous. At least I know I did, because Bud looked downright stupefied. His jaw hung slack and the whites of his eyes showed like a cartoon character in shock. I probably was worse, because Bud recovered enough to speak first.

"You know, that is just too nice, Miss Henderson. We wouldn't tell a soul, that's for sure."

"Not a soul," I mimicked stupidly.

"Good," she said with a curt shake of her head. "If you boys will just follow me, I'll take you to my spot. Come on, Brutus, you can go too."

The bear snorted and walked placidly along with us, just as if he had understood every word. We were afraid to speak, concerned that some kind of spell would be broken and Flossie would suddenly remember that this wonderful secret could never be shared. We walked to the edge of the creek and turned away from the bridge. About a hundred yards down we saw a large, flat clearing covered with grass. Flossie pointed to it and raised her eyebrows.

"There it is. My secret fishing hole. You boys have to promise not to keep the small ones and don't keep more than what you'll eat."

"Yes, Ma'am," we chorused.

"Oh, and you have to feed some of your fish to Brutus. Now that he knows you, he'll not try to chase you anymore. Actually, I don't believe he would have harmed you anyway. But," she added with a raised finger of warning, "don't deny him a fish if he really wants it. He can, you know, get testy."

"No problem," I promised, with Bud nearly shaking his head off in agreement. We were itching to get our lines into the water.

"Use this for bait," she added, and pulled out four slices of bread from her tackle box. "Take a piece like this," she tore a half inch piece from the length of the bread slice, "and mix a bit of dirt into it. That way the bread won't dissolve into the water."

"Thank you," I said, wanting to get at those fish. "Should we know anything else?"

"No, I think that should do it," Flossie said with a small grim. "Now, if you boys will excuse me, I usually take a nap in the afternoon." She began moving back downstream without waiting for us to comment.

"Thanks again," I called out when she was about to round a bend in the creek. We had almost forgotten her in our haste to begin fishing.

Brutus flopped down near us like a huge dog, obviously waiting for the first fish. He soon grew tired of the wait and rolled to one side, instantly beginning to snore. About an hour passed without so much as a nibble. Bud smoked another cigarette but I declined, somewhat realizing that I didn't really like it, the sixties rebellion being a weak motivation.

"What's the deal here?" Bud growled. "We got

nothin' here, yet Flossie had a stringer full of fish."

"I'm beginning to think we've been had," I agreed. "This probably is not her spot at all. Think about it, Bud. Why would Flossie give up her spot to two kids? She was putting us on."

"Well, maybe she figures it's time to pass the secret along," Bud reasoned. "After all, she's old. She could die any minute, and then the secret is gone." He looked at me in dismay. "Maybe they just aren't biting today."

"Yeah, that's why Flossie had a stringer full earlier," I said. "We've been had, Bud."

Brutus must have sensed the same, because he grunted, rolled to his feet, yawned mightily, and lumbered off into the brush. Even he gave up any hope of getting another fish.

"Let's try worms," Bud suggested. "Maybe it's the right spot but the bread isn't working."

"We can change depth, too," I added, clinging to some false hope.

The day wore on, finally reaching the time for us to leave. We gathered our equipment and trudged sadly toward the bridge. We tried one more time to see the hidden path under the clover, but either the shifting sun or the few hours of growth covered the telltale clue. We probably lost our one moment to follow it to the true fishing hole.

"Well, at least we didn't get killed by that bear," Bud reflected.

"And we're no worse off now than before," I added, though without much conviction.

"We've got quite an experience to remember," Bud said, "something we'll both always remember."

"Why, Bud," I said, sincerely astonished. "I had no idea you had any sentimental feelings."

He blushed, genuinely embarrassed. "Yeah,

well don't broadcast it, okay?" he growled with false bravado.

We didn't talk again until my mother came to pick us up. Bud insisted that he could walk home but of course my mother wouldn't hear of it.

"Thanks," he said when we pulled into the Campbell's gravel drive. The front screen door hung askew with one hinge missing and the paint was more than half gone from the warped clapboard siding. One window had a large hole in it and another was missing completely. Bud seemed embarrassed although nothing was said. "Hey, Bill," he added as he pushed the car door shut, "this was fun. Really. Maybe we can do it again sometime." He was off with a trot, dust puffing up from the gravel at each step like exhaust from a muffler.

"Well," my mother said with a smile, "it sounds like you boys had an eventful day even though you didn't catch any fish."

"You know how it is," I said quietly, "when you put your life on the line with a guy you tend to look at things differently."

"What on earth do you mean by that?" she said, twisting in the car seat to study me carefully.

"Oh, nothing. You know, just kid stuff."

Chapter 15

Aunt Edie recovered from the surgery itself quite
rapidly. She was weak, but I expected that as a
result of her ordeal. I don't think I wanted to ask,
nor did I want to know, if her weakness could be
related to cancer that was still in her body.

I was amazed at the arsenal of medicine. She
was a walking drug store, a measure which Uncle
Eddie determined was intended by her doctors to "run
up the bill." There were pills to help her sleep at night.
There were pills to wake her in the morning. One pill
was a diuretic for the kidneys while another helped
retain fluids to prevent dehydration.

"Look at this," she said one morning. " I take
thirty seven pills before breakfast, twenty at noon,
and another forty seven at bed time. I don't have
any room for food."

"Maybe you don't need food with all of those
pills," I suggested. "You could work for the circus
in the side show. We'll call you pill woman."

She laughed, a sound I came to treasure as the
weeks moved on. She winced and touched her still
swollen stomach, then laughed again. "Oh, it hurts
when I laugh," she said.

"Then don't laugh," I suggested, alarmed by her
pain.

"If I can't laugh, then there's no reason to live," she replied.

"And you've got a lot of reasons to live."

"Absolutely," she declared, shifting her mood to the lighter side and laughing again.

She swung her legs from the bed and slid slender feet into slippers with roses embroidered on the top. Her legs were as white as linen, and ugly blue veins rose to the surface like worms after a hard rain. Red sores like irritated eyes stood out in stark contrast on her legs, a dab of ointment on each serving as a benign attempt of a cure.

"Help me to get outside," she said. "I need some fresh air and a short walk."

I took her gently by the elbow, shocked at the trembling I felt. She winked at me and we moved slowly through the dining room and out the back door. The wheat field in back whispered gently in the wind, the sound bringing a smile to her lips.

"Oh look." She moved slowly toward a low growing bush at the corner of our house. "Isn't that a bird nest?"

I walked in slow motion beside her, seeing the small nest buried within the evergreen's branches. "It's a bush wren. We get several nests every year. They don't do too well because the cat usually gets them. They live in the thickets along the fence rows, but some find a spot in our bushes."

"The cat gets them?" She seemed upset at the thought.

"It sure does," I said. "Rick says that's what happens when they try to live around people. The world eats you up."

"Yes, I suppose so," she said thoughtfully. "The world does tend to eat us up, doesn't it?"

"Not the tough ones like you," I answered, understanding her meaning. "You're too tough."

"That I am," she agreed. "Let's sit on the steps for a minute while I catch my breath, okay?" She looked wistfully at the empty nest and walked carefully to the concrete steps.

I was afraid that maybe I would be uneasy around her, not knowing what to say or do. The reverse turned out to be true. I realized I could say anything to my aunt, and I had a very peaceful feeling that I could help her. She must have felt the same, because she asked for my company often while she stayed with us.

We settled ourselves on the cool but hard cement and were both quiet for some time. "Billy," she said, without turning her eyes toward me, "am I going to die?"

"I told you before, no," I declared. "That option is not available."

"I'm sorry. You're so young. I have no right to burden you."

"Aunt Edie, you always told people that Rick and I are your kids, too. How could you be a burden on me?"

Her eyes filled with tears and she swiped them away angrily with the back of her hand. "I'm so scared," she said. "It's not right to be scared."

"It is too," I declared. I put an arm around her shoulders and felt her bony shoulders through the gown that she wore. "I don't think it would be normal to feel any other way."

"Well, this is stupid." She sighed heavily. "Remember, feeling sorry for yourself does not make good sense. Use your efforts to accomplish things, things that will help others. If you do good works your life will be remembered. Can you understand what I mean?" Her tears escaped and slid down her cheeks.

"I do. I just want you to be around while I grow

up. Selfish aren't I?" I said.

She laughed a bit through her tears. "Well, be selfish all you want."

We were quiet again for a while, just sitting there listening to birds singing and the wind gently blowing through the wheat. "Can I tell you something that's kind of weird?" I asked.

"Of course, Billy" she answered, suddenly very attentive. "You can tell me anything."

"I mean, something I don't want to tell anyone else. You know, like I'm telling a preacher or a lawyer."

I suppose this sounded absurd, but she didn't change expressions. A robin flew to the ground about three feet from us, and we both froze in place as it watched us for a long moment. She slowly put her hand in the pocket of her robe and pulled out a soda cracker. Gently flipping it toward the bird, the robin flew away in fear.

"Did you see how that robin ran away from the help I wanted to give it?" she asked, one eyebrow arched upward in emphasis. "If I told anyone something you asked me not to repeat, why wouldn't you react the same as that robin if you ever wanted help from me again?"

"So you won't tell." Despite her analogy, I needed to hear her say the words.

Her face flinched as a stab of pain scampered across her swollen stomach, then she recovered and patted my knee. "No, I won't tell"

"I play basketball by myself."

She looked at me like I was still going to tell her what my problem was. "Yes."

"Well, that's it. I have teams and everything. I play games to fifty, keep score by player, and keep league standings and all of that." I looked at her closely, waiting for a horrified expression before she told me I was nuts.

"So, you're saying you play pretend basketball games against other teams."

"Yeah." My head hung in shame.

"Billy, let me ask you something. Why did you tell me this?"

"Well, it's been bothering me, you know. I figured that I must be weird to do this, and I just needed to tell you."

She paused in thought, carefully choosing her words. "Will you trust what I tell you?" she inquired.

"Sure,," I said without hesitation. "I wouldn't have told you it I didn't trust what you say."

"Good. Then listen carefully." She narrowed her eyes sternly, looking like the tough aunt that demanded work on her flower beds. "I don't want to make light of this, Billy, because it obviously bothers you. But frankly, there is nothing wrong with your pretend games."

I was stunned. I expected to be told that I was one step away from being locked up for the rest of my life, and now I'm told it's no big deal. "You've been worried about nothing."

"You're not just saying that because you don't want me to feel bad?"

"Nope. Look, Billy, I may not be around that much longer. A person in my position can't afford to lie when it comes to thinking about answering for things that are wrong. I don't want a bunch of lies on my conscience."

"Wow," I breathed, relief flooding through me like warm water. "I really thought I had a problem."

"Well, you don't," she said with a note of finality. "Play your heart out, Honey. Some day you won't think life is a game, treat it as such for as long as possible." She pushed her way to her feet. "Now come on, help me back inside and you can get me some orange juice."

After that I played my games with abandon and enjoyed them completely.

Chapter 16

My summer moved along slowly, being typically wasted as only youth can do. I wouldn't understand until years later how important those lazy days were, and yet I don't know if I would have changed a thing. My parents thought I was bothering Aunt Edie, and I imagine that was a fact.

A local nurseryman hired boys during the summer to hoe fields of young plants and to dig mature stock for planting in yards. My father asked him to give me a try, which he readily agreed to do. I soon discovered that Earl Long was to teach me more about the work ethic than any person I have ever known. He paid me one dollar an hour, and it was the toughest dollar I ever earned.

There was nothing very unusual about the man, at least not as you looked at him. He stood about five foot ten inches tall and weighed about one hundred sixty pounds. His hair was black and usually tousled from the wind. I never saw him dressed in a suit, as he nearly always wore dark green work pants and a plaid shirt in a variety of colors. His shoes were Red Wing steel-toed utility oxfords, and I don't believe he ever polished them or wore a different pair at any time that I worked for him. One eye was made of glass, an accident of youth that resulted from a stick gouging the eye from his head. He once told me that he had never felt pain of any kind in his life that had matched that day. A rare disease caused by a virus usually carried by pigeons left him night blind, which meant driving after dark was an extreme hazard.

Earl loved to teach young people about life. He owned Billy goats to teach us caution, because a turned back meant a hard butt in the, uhm, butt. He owned a peacock named Homer to teach us beauty, and the vanity that sometimes accompanies it. Cats were everywhere, each lovingly named and given a few minutes of his attention every day.

I arrived for my first day of work, a bit nervous, not knowing what to expect or how to react. Earl came from his house, which was a small ranch style with cedar siding. It rested at the top of a small hill and overlooked a greenhouse about twice its size. My father greeted him with a smile and they chatted for a few minutes. They walked over to me for the awkward first introduction.

"Billy, this is Mr. Long," my father said, using the dreaded "Billy".

"Hello, Bill. I'm Earl." He thrust out his hand and smiled, showing a line of even, pearl white teeth. He said Bill! I knew instantly I would like this man.

"Hi, nice to meet you," I said shyly.

"Well, I've got to be off to work myself," my father said. "Mom will pick you up at four," he added.

"Okay. Have a good day," I replied.

Earl didn't speak again until we waved at my father pulling onto the road and heading for the factory. He put a hand that felt like leather wrapped in sandpaper on the back of my neck and winked with his one good eye. "Ready to go to work?" This was a statement, not a question, so I did not answer. "Grab that long-handled hoe over there and come with me."

He pointed to a disorganized pile of shovels, rakes, spades, and hoes, then strode away with a strong purpose. I snatched up a hoe that looked like it had the largest handle and ran after my new boss. He was, I would guess, in his middle forties, and he moved with the grace of a deer and the strength of a bear. We walked down a dusty pathway, lined on each side by small pine trees. About a quarter of a mile down the path we came to an old wooden fence that surrounded a five acre field of small landscape plants. I discovered later, as my experience increased, that there were several varieties of taxus, as well as juniper and burning bushes in the field. He paused at the gate, me panting and sweating, he cool, composed, and breathing easily.

"You tired already?" he asked. Before I could reply, he held up a finger to silence any answer. "Watch this," he said, and pulled a nail from his pants pocket. He positioned the tip on the top of the fence post that held the gate at its entrance. With his thumb he easily pushed the nail half way into the wooden post. "Now, you pull it out," he challenged.

I looked at that nail dumbly, trying to figure out the trick. "Just pull it out."

"Right. Just grab the nail and pull it out of the post. Go ahead," he added in encouragement.

With a shrug, I grabbed the nail in a firm grip and pulled. Nothing happened. I grinned, nostrils flaring, and pulled harder. My fingers slid to the top of the nail and it cut painfully into my flesh. I relaxed my grip and wiped my hand on my pants. Mentally I pictured the nail out of the post and tried again. The nail did not move.

Earl reached out and took the nail between his thumb and middle finger. He effortlessly pulled it out and stuck the nail back into his pocket. "Do you see that field?" he asked.

"Yes, sir, I do" I mumbled, awed by what he had just done. I was staring at the small hole left by the nail.

"Hoe around these plants and I'll come tell you when to quit. If you do that kind of work for enough years, some day you'll be able to do what I just did." He started down the dusty path, then paused and looked back. "But don't do this kind of work long enough to ever be able to do that," he added, and strode away.

That was one of the longest days of my life. The sun beat my back like a hot whip, aided by ninety percent Ohio humidity. I wanted to make a good impression, so my work pace was close to a frenzy. Within minutes I was stripped to the waist, and sweat riveted down to soak my Levi jeans. I had nothing but that hoe. No food, water, or even a hat. Time flew by without measure.

I barely even looked up as I worked, and each weed fell as the sharp blade dug into the hard ground and sliced under the unyielding plant, removing the root system as well. I sensed, rather than heard, someone's presence. I looked over my shoulder and saw Earl standing by the gate, a large wicker basket held in one hand.

"Well, you've done some work," he said with a smile.

I looked about for the first time, and noticed with some surprise that almost half of the field was hoed.

"The last fellow that worked this field took two days to finish. You've got a shot at being done today. If you can keep up the pace." he added. "We'll see if you're twice as good as he is. But for the moment, come over here. I've got some things for you."

I walked over to the fence as he opened the top of the basket. He pulled out a gallon jug made of clear glass. It was full of water. He handed it to me without comment, so without asking I unscrewed the rusted metal cap and drank. The water was cool and fresh, and I had never tasted anything more wonderful.

"Don't go too fast of you'll bring it up," he cautioned. "Save some for a bit later."

I lowered the jug and replaced the cap. I had chugged nearly half of the gallon. He handed me a wax paper wrapped bologna sandwich that I wolfed down in three bites. A second sandwich went down in similar fashion. Yet a third went slower, but I still ate every crumb. He finished by handing me two peaches and a banana. At last I felt like I would continue to live.

"Now, turn around and I'll put some of this on your back," he said, producing a bottle of Coppertone suntan lotion. The little girl on the front of the bottle that was getting her swim suit pulled down by the dog looked over her shoulder with surprise. She seemed to be horrified by my sunburn, not the little dog. "And put this on," he added, handing me a straw hat with a wide brim. "Tomorrow, have your mom put lotion on your back, bring a big jug of water, and don't forget your lunch. Get your fresh water from the greenhouse pump. It's the best well water you'll ever drink. And you can keep the hat. It was left here by an employee that never came back." He started down the path again, basket in hand. "I'll be back around six. If you finish the field, just rest in the shade." He was gone in an instant.

I attacked the field with a vengeance. Weeds flew right and left, silently yielding to the stroke of my hoe's deadly blade. I blinked sweat from my eyes, watering the dry ground with salty drops of perspiration. I stopped only twice, once to finish off the jug of water, and once to study the amount of field I had yet to finish.

I reached the last plant in the last row and finally my day's work was done. I could hear Earl's dusty shoes clomping rapidly down the dusty lane. Quickly I ran to a large maple tree near the path and stretched out under the shade of its large branches. I pulled the straw hat over my eyes and began to snore with gusto.

He stopped at my feet and stood there for some time. I opened one eye slightly and looked through the checkered pattern of the straw hat. He was looking over the field and nodding his head with obvious approval. Finally he tapped the sole of my shoe with his foot. "Wake up. It's time to go home."

I snorted and jumped, hopefully not too much to cause suspicion, and stretched like a cat. I added a huge yawn for maximum effect. "Oh, sorry. I guess I fell asleep," I said. "Is it six o'clock already?"

"Um hum" he said. "How long have you been done?"

"Gosh, I really don't know," I lied. "I don't have a watch. I just finished the job a while ago and lay in the shade like you told me. I must have been pretty tired since I fell asleep, but I have been resting for a while so I guess it's not too strange that I slept. Sorry." I stood, wanting to chuckle at the look on his face, but not daring to do so.

"No, no. Don't be sorry, you did just fine," he said, mystified. "I told you to rest in the shade after you finished the field. You just did what you were told to do." He walked away slowly, shaking his head. "You did a lot of work in a short time. You must be tired."

"Yes, sir, I guess I am," I answered. I became a legend that day at the Lost Hollow Nursery.

I soon got to know my way around the place, and discovered that I really liked the work. Earl took me with him to help do estimates on new jobs. I measured the area that was to be planted, and he showed me how to create drawings with plants labeled and positioned to scale. He began my education of what plants looked the best and did well in various conditions. Evergreens made excellent plants, while low growing pfitzers and euononmous gave color and beauty without growing tall and covering windows. My favorite was the bush honeysuckle that created a tall, natural fence and smelled like a sweet perfume. Earl's ability to mix the exact blend of plants together was nothing short of miraculous.

He owned a true nursery. Plants grew on a hundred acres of field which were scattered over three farms which Earl had purchased a number of years before. He owned four tractors of which two did not work on a rotating basis. Three old station wagons were usually full of burlap or freshly dug plants, and we boys drove all of the equipment like we were adults. Long hours of hot, dirty work were quickly forgotten when the opportunity to drive a car to one of the fields presented itself. My mother would have had a fit, but I think my father knew. Surely he must have wondered how, when I turned sixteen, I could drive our car from the first lesson like a professional.

Another fascinating thing was learning to ball and burlap a plant. A very sharp spade was used to cut the ground away from a plant or tree, being careful to leave enough dirt around the roots. This

was called the ball. The depth was also important,
as plants have a main, central root called the tap
root If it is cut too short, the plant will be stunted
or even die. Learning the correct size and depth
for each plant we dug was vital. The burlap came
into play after the plant was dug. A knife was used
to cut a piece to size, then it was wrapped around
the ball of dirt with the four corners at the top.
Opposite corners were pulled together and nails
were poked through the burlap on one side. The
protruding tip was stuck into the other corner ,
then the nail was pushed over so it changed direction, then it was shoved into the dirt. This method
pulled the burlap tight and made the nail hold like
a staple. The whole process worked amazingly well,
and the tree or plant could be handled easily
without fear of breaking the ball of dirt or harm-
ing the plant.

Large trees took several people to dig and handle. I saw tap roots as large as the leg of a man,
and they were about as difficult to cut. Sometimes
we had to tunnel our way to this root and chop
through it with an ax. Then we rolled the tree up
planks onto a flat bed wagon, which was then
pulled by tractor or car to the work site. A hole
about twice the size of the ball of dirt had to be
dug for replanting. The whole process was very
hard work, bur few plants died.

The days blended together quickly, and I had
new discoveries to tell Aunt Edie about each day.
She still looked weak and tired, but I was convinced she seemed better as time went on. I was
pretty excited about all that I had learned and she
seemed to enjoy sharing the experiences with me.

I worked until noon on Saturdays, another
proof that my job was agreeing with me. One such
day Earl and I had been working a job on Lima's

west side. We got back to the nursery around twelve thirty and my father was roaming about the greenhouse, looking at plants and basically just killing time until I returned.

"Sorry we're late, Kenny," Earl called out as we walked in, loaded with charts and plans for the new job.

"No problem," my father said with a smile and a wave to us both. "I was just admiring your handiwork."

"I start all my own plants from cuttings," Earl said with pride. "Besides saving an awful lot of money, I know my stock will always be top quality."

"And indeed it always has been," my father agreed with a shake of his head. "And how is my youngest doing?" He nodded in my direction.

Earl put his two work hardened thumbs into the air. "The boy's a natural. I've been thinking of asking him to buy in with me. If there were two of us we could lose money twice as fast." He winked solemnly and patted my shoulder.

"That's good," my father answered with a smile. "Sounds like a darn solid business plan, too."

They both laughed and obviously enjoyed the humor, which basically escaped me. I spotted a barn cat and went over to pet it while the two men talked. They chatted for another fifteen minutes before my father finally said we had to get home and take care of the farm chores before nightfall. I groaned inwardly but just smiled and left the purring cat.

We drove home fairly quietly, just enjoying being with each other and not finding it necessary to say that much. I had learned that my father accomplished more in a month in his quiet way than most men did in a lifetime of blustering about themselves. He believed that if you had to brag about your accomplishments then they weren't very important to anyone but yourself.

We cruised into our driveway and Rick came running toward the car, frantically waving his arms, My father stopped the car and waited for my brother to regain his composure enough to speak. Rick pointed toward the east, his voice still giving out because of his excitement. I noticed a large black cloud of smoke rising into the air about three miles away. Rick grabbed the car with both hands at the open window, his knuckles turning white from the grip. Finally he blurted out, " The Thornton's place in on fire."

Chapter 17

Lloyd and Ellen Thornton lived with their three children in a classic two story farm house about three miles to the east of our house. They were on Bluelick Road, but across the township line. The two boys went to Allen East Elementary School, and their sister at five years old would start school in a year. There was no kindergarten for kids in the country. We didn't know them really well, but my father saw Lloyd occasionally at the granary in Lafayette when the crops were harvested. The Thornton's were Catholic, so we didn't see them on Sundays at Liberty Chapel like nearly everyone else in the area.

Rick was pointing to the thick black smoke rising in the air in the distance. "How do you know it's the Thornton house?" my father asked. He got out of the car to better see the increasing cloud of smoke.

"Joe was on his bike and saw the smoke coming from the upstairs windows. He came by and we called the fire department."

"How long ago?" As he spoke, my father climbed back into the car.

"Just a minute ago. Joe headed back that way. Can I go?"

Without answering, my father put the car in reverse and virtually flew back onto the road. I had been sitting on the edge of the seat and the sudden movement threw me back into the cushions. The car shot forward with a squeal of the rear tires. I looked back and saw Rick running toward his bike. My father shifted when the engine wound tight, and more tire rubber was left on the pavement.

His face was mask of concentration and purpose. I don't believe I had ever seen him that intense. We flew through the stop sign at the corner of Bluelick and Kool Road without a glance, the car still accelerating. Joe was peddling his bicycle for all he was worth, and we came up on him in an instant. The blast of air as we rushed by made his front wheel wobble in protest and pulled the Cincinnati Reds hat from his head. Joe didn't even glance back at the hat laying on its top in the middle of the road. He just put his head down and peddled harder.

The Thornton house was coming up just around a bend in the road. I looked at the speedometer and saw the red needle quivering at the eighty mile per hour mark. Trees flashed by and leaves blew off branches that were close to the ground. A crow was standing in the road, pecking at a dead squirrel who had been run down by another vehicle. The bird looked up and arrogantly stared at our car, daring us to hit him. My father took the dare and blasted the horn in warning. The crow realized at the last moment that it had misjudged this huge machine, and flapped it's wings in panic as the car rushed on. We somehow missed the bird, but I'll never understand how. I saw the black creature flying toward the solitude and comparable safety of a large tree as we continued our frenzied path to the burning house.

We took the curve on two wheels, the car rocking right and then slamming down solidly on the pavement as my father recovered on the straightway. He leaned forward over the steering wheel as if he wanted to get there faster by being closer to the front of the car. He slammed his foot hard on the brake pedal and the car slid into the gravel driveway of the Thornton's barn. The house sat fifty yards to the right, and by now flames were licking out of the upstairs windows. My father turned off the engine and let out the clutch, the wheels locked as our car slid in the stones. He was out of the door before we completely stopped. The front of our car had slid toward Thornton's house providing me a perfect panoramic view of the fire without leaving my seat.

Ellen Thornton was huddled on the grass a safe distance from the flames, holding two hysterical boys. They clung to her like two primitive creatures and howled in fear. "Where are Lloyd and Sara?" my father screamed at her.

"Lloyd went in to find her," she said, gesturing toward the flames. "They haven't come out." she cried, tears streaming down her face.

Running toward the house, my father hesitated only to grab a garden hose attached to the house and, after turning on the faucet, soaked his head and clothes. He took off his shirt and wrapped it around his face. Soot pouring out of the house fell onto his white undershirt, spotting it with black dots. He ran to the open front door and disappeared inside. This made me move, and I jumped from the car and ran toward the garden hose.

The heat was so intense that the paint was blistering on the outside of the house. I dragged the hose full length away from the house, and waited for someone to come out. I locked the metal sprayer on the end of the hose full on, and water burst forth. It was hot for a full minute, then became warm. The hose had started to melt, but the water flow at least temporarily stopped that.

Joe came peddling fiercely into the front yard, leaping from his bike and running to where I stood with the hose. "Where's your dad?" he yelled over the noise of the flames.

"Inside," I answered. "Mr. Thornton and Sara are in there too."

Joe's eyes bulged and his jaw went slack. "They can't live in that."

"Don't say that!" I screamed. "My dad's in there and he has to come out."

Seemingly by my command my father stumbled from the burning house, carrying Mr. Thornton over his shoulder. Both men were in flames, the fire having ignited their clothing. I turned the hose on them as my father ran toward me, his burden bouncing like a burning bag of potatoes. Smoke poured from them like fog as the water quickly put out the fire.

"Mr. Keller," Joe yelled. "Are you okay?"

Coughing prevented him from answering. I just kept the water spraying on them both and finally Mr. Thornton moaned and started coughing too. "Got to get back in," my father gasped. "Sara must be upstairs."

"You can't," I cried. "The whole place is gone. You can't go in there again."

He had grabbed the hose from me and was soaking himself. "I've got to, son. I won't leave her in there." Before I could argue any more, he winked and ran back inside.

Mr. Thornton sat up, looking dazed and confused. Joe helped him to his feet and took him to his family. They all knelt on the lawn, holding each other. I could hear Mrs. Thornton praying. Rick came next, dropping his bike next to our cousin's. His face was flushed from the ride and the fire reflected brightly in his wide eyes. "I heard sirens a minute ago," he gasped. "But it looks like it's too late. There's no way they can save the house. Where's Dad?"

"In the house," I said. I quickly brought him up to date as to what had happened.

"He can't make it in there," Joe said as a section of the roof collapsed.

"He has to," I simply stated. Fear suddenly gripped my heart. Because of the excitement I hadn't really thought about my father not getting out of the inferno. A fire truck roared into the front yard, siren screaming in an ear splitting pitch. Six men jumped down and began pulling hoses free in preparation to fight a battle that was already lost. One man ran over to us and asked, " Is anyone inside?"

"My father is trying to find Sara Thornton," I said, my voice trembling. "He just brought out Mr. Thornton."

The fire fighter glanced at the family, still huddled together. "Where do you think they are in there?" he asked.

"Right there!" Rick cried out. He was pointing at my father, who was carrying a bundle wrapped in a blanket He had run out the front door just as the entire front of the house collapsed in a shower of sparks and flames.

Smoke bounced like dust from his head as he ran toward the hose, and I tilted the sprayer up to help it hit him an instant sooner. He gasped as the droplets hit his scorched skin. The firefighter grabbed Sara from his arms and began blowing air into her lungs. She almost immediately started crying.

"I'm afraid I got burned," my father said quietly and then crumpled to the ground.

Two firefighters, who were also paramedics, rushed to his side. The others were hooking up hoses and preparing to use the truck's water tanks to fight the losing cause. The house was lost, as the roof had now caved in and the walls crumpled inward, consumed by the fire.

My attention was riveted to my father, who was coughing and gasping for breath. An oxygen mask was placed over his mouth, which seemed to help. Blisters were on his hands, arms and face. He looked like he had fallen asleep in the sun. Most of the hair on his head was burned off near to the scalp, and even his eyebrows had burned away. I couldn't see him very clearly, then realized it was because of the tears in my eyes mixing with the soot from the fire.

He looked at me and smiled through the oxygen mask, his eyes and teeth looking like white islands in the smoky dirt of his face. His eyes kept getting wider and then returned to normal, and I realized with comic horror that he was wiggling his eyebrows at me. I didn't understand at first because they were gone. A rescue squad came to the scene, and ultimately my father was the only one taken to the hospital. The Thornton's, thanks to my father, were fine except for the loss of their home. They often said in later years that their loss was nothing, thanks to Kenny Keller.

Chapter 18

Three days later my father came home. He looked like Lon Chaney in The Mummy, but all his burns would heal and leave virtually no scars. The newspapers made a pretty big deal about his heroism, but my father, in his typical quiet way, wanted no part of the attention. He insisted that no copies of *The Lima News* be kept, but I think my mother asked some people from church to give her copies of the article which she hid away.

The very day my father came home from the hospital, Aunt Edie went back into the hospital. She scared us half out of our wits in the process, because her temperature spiked to one hundred and four. It happened so fast that she went into convulsions and swallowed her tongue. My mother pried open her mouth and pulled it from the back of her throat, which saved her life.

Rick called the rescue squad, and they took her to Memorial Hospital. Even though it him hurt to move too much, my father drove Rick and me to the hospital because we had to know what was happening. We found my mother pacing in the surgery waiting area. She sat on the edge of a straight-backed chair and when we came in explained the situation.

"She had a very bad infection. They thought it had to be related to the surgery, so they went in to find the problem." She paused and blinked back tears. Her hands wound around a white cotton handkerchief, pulling it to the point of tearing. "There was a spot that was full of infection, so they took it out. They also found...they found," she cleared her throat and swallowed hard, "more cancer."

"How did they miss that before?" I asked incredulously.

"It wasn't there before," she said bluntly.

"So they just have to take it out," said Rick with false confidence. He looked at us and nodded his head vigorously as if that would help us to agree.

"They said she probably has more that they can't see. Doctor Fleckner said it's likely that she's full of cancer." She stood and began to pace again.

My father sat carefully on a vinyl sofa, trying to get as comfortable as his burns would allow. He frowned and considered out loud, "Then she should try radiation or chemical treatment. There have been some wonderful advancements made."

"I suppose Dr. Fleckner will talk about those things," my mother agreed. "He wanted to check some test results before suggesting anything else."

"Where's Eddie?" my father wondered.

"He's on his way. I found him at work and he said he wouldn't even go home first." Mother shook her head sadly. "This is tearing him up. He's been talking about quitting his job and coming back to Lima."

"I can understand how he feels," my father agreed, "but he can't give up a good job in today's economy. He'll be in a mess soon."

"I know, that's what we talked about when he

was transferred. He was just upset. He's feeling guilty and angry right now. This is just something he'll have to work through."

There seemed to be nothing more to say, so we sat quietly and waited. My father was still pretty tired from his ordeal and dozed as my mother periodically paced around the room. Uncle Eddie arrived about two hours later, an indication that he had broken several major traffic laws during his drive from Detroit. He was white with shock when he heard the details of Aunt Edie's condition.

"That's it," he said, more in concern than anger, "I'm coming back home."

"Don't decide anything until you think it through and talk to Dr. Fleckner," my father counseled.

"I can't handle this," he replied, and put shaking hands over his face. My mother hugged him and he buried his face on her shoulder.

Dr. Fleckner limped into the waiting room eight hours after the surgery began. He looked exhausted, and I noted that his huge hands were still raw from scrubbing and hours of wearing latex gloves. He still wore a blue surgical gown and the thin hat that kept hair from falling into his patient's open wounds during surgery. Padded slippers covered his shoes, like pontoon boats instead of feet. He looked sad, like a man who did not like his job but had to accept the responsibility of its position. All eyes were on him, making his shoulders slump a bit farther. There was no one in that room who could have said anything to make us turn our attention from this huge man.

"She's out of surgery," he began without preliminary small talk. "I took out some badly infected tissue, which should bring her temperature down almost immediately." He looked at his hands and picked at a patch of dry skin. "I removed seven tumors that were not there when she had surgery before. That means that what I saw earlier I can confirm now." He paused to let us digest what he had said.

"Are you sure that it was more...cancer?" Uncle Eddie asked.

"Of course we'll get a full lab report, Eddie, but because we know the other tumors were malignant it is pretty likely that these are too. I've seen enough of both, and I can pretty much tell that these are not benign."

"Then, is there anything we can do?" he asked, the strain showing in his face.

The doctor looked down at the floor and studied the pattern in the tile. "There is always a chance that we got everything. I took every tumor that I saw."

"But what do you think?" Uncle Eddie persisted. I could see in his eyes that he knew the answer, but was hoping for a different answer.

"I don't think," the doctor hesitated, biting his lower lip, "that it is very likely that we could have found all of the malignancy."

"Then what do we do?" he asked, his voice pinched and raspy.

"We make her as comfortable and keep her as free as possible from pain." The doctor was looking into Uncle Eddie's eyes. "Do you understand?"

Tears ran down his cheeks, but his voice was now clear and firm. "Yes, I understand, Doctor Fleckner." He held the tired eyes with his own.

"Remember, I may have removed all of the cancer," he repeated. "We won't know for weeks or even months."

"Fine. Thank you for helping her," Uncle Eddie

said. The tears still cascaded down his cheeks, but the expression did not change, nor did he seem to notice.

"We'll all pray for her," Dr. Fleckner said and limped from the room.

Chapter 19

Summer was nearing the end. After three weeks in the hospital Aunt Edie came home, and life kind of returned to normal. She became an audience of one, or should I say two, counting Daisy, in watching me play my pretend basketball games. She even kept score for me as I called out the player credited with making the score, and occasionally I permitted her to decide who made each basket. The problem with that method was that she counted most of the points to me and made my stats even more lopsided than before. Actually, I didn't really care because she was with me.

She seemed to be getting better, the swelling in her stomach going down and her color returning to a healthy shine. While acting as my official statistician she sat in the sun, adding a healthy looking brown to her skin. Even her legs lost the ugly sores and darkened under the warm sun. There was even talk that maybe she could take care of herself in Detroit. Uncle Eddie was basically going bat crackers, which was as close as my mother would permit anyone to say the real thing. He was working out a leave of absence, but the bureaucratic wheels were moving slowly. He had so far agreed to keep his job and came to Lima every weekend

Working filled a lot of my time, but when the weather turned rainy the ground was too wet to work at the garden center. This was all right with me, because I wanted to be with Aunt Edie for as much time as possible. School would be starting soon and I knew that would be the end of my lazy days.

I had just finished my third game of one-on-one basketball when Aunt Edie waved me over. She did everything but call a moving company to haul all of her equipment each time she left the bed in our living room. She sat in a webbed lawn chair surrounded by a cooler full of home made grape juice, a beach bag with sun glasses, Coppertone, Vaseline, Nutrigena hand creme, a straw hat, and her medicine chest. It contained over fifty bottles of pills, each one taken several times every day. I swear I don't know how she ate with all of the stuff filling her stomach. Usually, she also brought out a hassock to prop her feet on, preventing swelling of the ankles or phlebitis.

I ran to her, out of breath and sweaty, overall feeling great. She smiled and reached out her hand, which I took. It felt hollow, like the wing of a bird. Automatically I held it gently, like an egg with a thin shell.

"I've got an idea," she said. "Why don't we take a walk."

"Sure," I readily agreed. "How about once around the barn and back."

"No." she shook her head firmly. "I want to walk in the woods."

I looked at her dubiously, then glanced toward the trees at the rear of the fifty acre field behind our house. "That's kind of far, don't you think? Maybe I could take you back on the tractor."

"The tractor would shake me apart," she replied. "We'll have to walk."

"I don't know..." I began.

"Billy, I want to smell the woods dirt. I want to sift it through my fingers. I want to look at the sun shining through the leaves. I want to watch Daisy chase squirrels. I want, oh, I just want." She shrugged, knowing there was really no more to say.

"Maybe we should wait until you're stronger," I persisted. "Maybe another few weeks."

She looked into my eyes. I saw sadness, pain, and knowledge. I saw no fear. "I have something growing in me. I can feel it getting bigger and stronger. Billy, I don't have a few weeks to wait for a walk in the woods."

I dropped my eyes, sorrow pressing hard against my chest. "I'll carry your things. Let's go."

We put three bottles of grape juice into the beach bag and did not take the cooler. I slung the beach bag and the chest full of pills over my right shoulder. I folded her chair and carried it in my left hand. The sun hovered over us in a cloudless sky and baked us like apples in the oven.

"Daisy," I yelled and added an ear piercing whistle. She came flying around the corner so fast that her missing rear leg counterbalanced the turn and she went rolling like a fur covered snowball. In one motion she flew to her feet and charged to me, slamming against my legs and knocking me and my carefully adjusted burden to the ground. Daisy leaped onto my chest and began licking my face, high yelps and whines coming from deep in her throat. Her tail wagged so hard that her rear end again lost its balance and flopped hard on my stomach. I whooshed loudly as air shot from my lungs, my legs flying involuntarily into the air.

I shoved the excited animal off me and sat up. In horror I saw Aunt Edie bent almost double, her arms crossed over her stomach. She bent her knees until they almost touched the blacktop driveway. Scrambling to my feet I ran to her, Daisy still excitedly tangling into my legs. I dropped to my knees in front of her and prepared to help her lay down until I could get help.

She was laughing, laughing so hard that her breath was gone again. Finally she stood and whooped like an Indian doing a war dance. Even through I was the reason for her tirade, I began laughing with her. She threw her arms around me, more for support than affection, and we shook with laughter for a full five minutes.

"I've never seen a three legged dog hit someone like a linebacker," she said, and promptly got the giggles again. "She took you down like a knight in a joust." Aunt Edie reached down and scratched Daisy's ears. The dog whined in ecstasy.

"She gets carried away," I agreed.

"Wow, I'll say," Aunt Edie said, composed once again. "Well, if we can all control ourselves, let's try to get started."

I gathered up all of our gear once again and we began our trek. The going was slow, because Aunt Edie was weaker than either of us realized. About every fifty yards or so I set up the chair and she rested for a short time. I fanned her flushed face and gave her a few pills as she directed from the medicine case.

"I'm sorry I got you into this," she gasped when we were a little over half way there. "I just wanted to do this in a really bad way."

"We will," I encouraged. "There is nothing we can't do if we put our minds to it. Look over there," I said and gestured to the edge of the woods, "we're almost there."

"Then let's get to it," she said bravely. "The

squirrels await, don't they Daisy?"

Daisy jumped at the sound of her name and led the way. We were in the shade of the oak and maple trees after two more rest stops, and then we moved a bit closer to the center. True to her part in my aunt's wish, Daisy chased squirrel after squirrel into trees, barking and yelping with glee. The trees seemed to be talking with the number of angry little bush tailed rodents chattering indignantly.

We laughed at her antics and I loved seeing Aunt Edie's smile. She sat in her chair like a woodland princess, pointing out birds and showing me different leaf formations. Daisy had grown tired and sat like a three legged lion at her feet, panting contentedly with her eyes half closed. Life was teeming around Aunt Edie, and she pushed over small branches on the ground to see bugs scurrying for shelter. She dug her toe into the deep bed of rotted leaves, bringing up worms and ants along with the musky scent of compost. Nothing was wasted in the woods, as all materials were eaten or used for shelter. Even empty nut shells discarded by the squirrels became home for small insects. Things died out here, but they lived on because they served a purpose.

"Look how the sun pushes through the leaves," she said. "You can see the beams of light coming through in a slant. If we were circus performers we could walk up like it was a wire. When we reached the top we would be close to the sun, then we could balance ourselves and look down at the earth." She raised her arms to the sky, trying to get closer to her fantasy. I held my breath as I watched, not wanting to break the spell that she was under. "I can almost touch a beam of light," she continued. "It's like a thread."

Her arms came down like they were slapped by a huge hand. The soft look on her face disappeared, her tranquil gaze flickered out like a candle in the wind. Pain replaced them all, grinding and stabbing its way into her midsection. "Pills," she gasped, biting hard on her lower lip. Blood trickled down and dripped off her chin. "Fast," she cried, spraying my hands with saliva diluted specks of blood from her torn lip.

I scrambled to her medicine chest and flung back the lid. All of the bottles looked the same to me, and their names were long unpronounceable words that I did not understand. I set the whole thing on her knees and looked dumbly into her pain contorted face, not knowing what to do. Her hands were bent like claws, the pain in her stomach affecting every fiber of her body. She pawed at the bottles, gasping small breaths of air through gritted teeth, her torn lip whistling slightly as her breath whooshed out. After finding the bottle she needed, Aunt Edie grunted, almost screamed and hit it with her knuckles. I snatched it up and tore off the cap, sending a small shower of pills so the ground as I shook one into my hand. She opened her mouth and I put one on her tongue, jerking my fingers away as her jaw spasmed shut. I reached for a bottle of grape juice and rummaged frantically for the opener to pop off the cap. She grabbed the bottle from me and in one motion hit its neck against a tree, snapping the slender top. Grape juice splashed onto her clothes as she threw her head back and sloshed juice into her mouth. She swallowed hard and closed her eyes, moaning in pain.

Around ten minutes later she began to slowly relax. The pain was still there, I saw it as her eyes opened, but she was managing it. She had regained control. "One more." She nodded at the bottle of pills, her voice a hoarse croak.

I shook out another pill and this time she took it from me with her fingers, popping it into her mouth, and washing it down in one quick motion. "I bit my lip," she rasped, looking at the blood.

"It's not bad," I said. "The bleeding is almost stopped. You sure look a mess though."

She chuckled, a drug-induced glaze showing in her now watery eyes. "I'm going to draw bees. I've got sticky grape juice all over me."

We sat silently for a while, she clearing her mind of the pain and I recovering from the shock and fear of her episode. Daisy had rested long enough and went back to chasing squirrels, but the fun and magic was gone so we really didn't pay attention to her. I think Aunt Edie dozed for a while, because her chin drooped to her chest. I sat with my back against a tree, my thoughts troubled and insecure.

Shadows were lengthening, a sign that the day was fading. Everything had a different perspective in the woods, and time had a way of slipping by unnoticed. I leaned forward and gently touched her knee, which brought her head up and she smiled. "This has been nice," she said, as if the attack of pain had never happened.

"We should head back," I said gently. "We don't want to get stuck out here after dark."

She nodded, automatically putting her hands to her hair in an attempt to freshen herself. Covered with blood and grape juice, her efforts were mostly wasted, but it seemed to make her feel better. She rose shakily to her feet as I gathered up our things and we started home.

"What is this?" she asked as we stopped near the edge of the woods for a rest. She was looking at a pile of junk and trash, some of it buried in old leaves and underbrush. She picked up an old paint can and looked at the label as if it could tell her something.

"This is stuff we throw away and bring back here to get rid of it," I answered. "This saves us a dumping fee at the county landfill. We burn paper and throw garbage in the field or the garden to rot away. I like coming here because I can remember things from the old days."

Aunt Edie smiled. "You're a bit young to be talking about the old days aren't you?"

"Yeah, I suppose so," I admitted. "But, you know they're the only old days I have."

She laughed and nodded her head in agreement. "I guess it's all perspective. Show me some memories."

I kicked through the junk and found a tricycle, its once beautiful chrome finish covered with rust. The solid rubber tires were mostly rotted away, with some globs of it still clinging at spots on the rims. "This was my first bike," I said. "It was blue and had a plastic horn on the handlebars. I think that horn lasted about a week before it went missing. I've always been convinced Rick threw it away but he always denied it. I don't know why, because I would have trashed the noisy thing, too, if it had been his."

"He didn't do it," Aunt Edie said with a smile.

"How do you know?" I innocently asked, being pretty slow of wit if you know what I mean.

"You went everywhere with that bike. It was at my house as much as yours." She raised her eyebrows and shrugged. "I hated that blasted horn. It went in our incinerator with the rest of the trash."

I laughed heartily at the thought. "I know you too well. You felt guilty and probably would have let this bother you forever. I'm glad you told me so it's off your back, Aunt Edie."

"Why do you think I bought you boys that new swing set when it wasn't even Christmas or a birthday?"

We laughed together. "A swing set for a ten cent horn," I hooted. "What a deal!"

"Oh, be quiet and show me something else," she said in a lame attempt to be stern.

"Here's an old toy tractor with a manure spreader," I announced, holding up two more treasures.

"Your mom told Uncle Eddie she knew exactly why he picked a manure spreader," she said. "She was right too. He's an ornery one you know." Speaking of him seemed to make her sad, and she looked away toward the house.

"Well, let's get going," I suggested, throwing the broken toys back onto the trash pile. "We can go slow if we start now."

"And slow it must be," she said and stood to go. "But at least I'm on my feet," she added.

We moved slowly back to our house. My mother saw us coming and came out to help. She started to be upset when she saw the dried blood and grape stains, but Aunt Edie told her she was fine and had just enjoyed one of the best days of her life. This closed the subject. Walking gingerly in the house, I saw how hard it was for her to keep going. I stayed outside until dark, laying in the grass and petting Daisy.

Chapter 20

The county fair came each year just before school started in late August. Since I had been working at Earl's nursery I had some money to spend, and the fair was the perfect place. I had always relied upon handouts from my parents, whose idea of plenty to spend was five dollars, not including the one dollar admission. This year I had twelve dollars set aside for the event, and I planned to experience the greatest fair in the history of man.

I called a friend of mine from school, Dave Koenig, whose brother Tom was sixteen and usually agreed, for a price, to take Dave places providing it was not inconvenient. Since everyone, including Tom Koenig, went to the county fair, and because he did not have to pretend to be with us, the small sum of fifty cents each bought our ride to the fair. The fair was considered safe by most parents, so we were allowed to go without adult supervision, providing there were at least two of us together. I was so excited I trembled as I waited for them to pick me up early Saturday morning for the opening day of the fair.

We didn't even talk much as we pulled from our drive and we headed for our day of fun. Tom's 1950 Ford coughed and choked, but it did run.

His tires were bald as the proverbial cue ball, and they sang as his speedometer topped sixty. The parking lot was reached without incident and in moments we were out of the car, Tom heading in one direction, Dave and I in another.

"Check it out," he cried at the Ferris wheel and the smell of the food stands. "What do we do first?" He deferred to me as I was the one with twelve dollars.

"I want to walk the grounds and see what's here," I said, which was my favorite way to take in the fair. It was especially great to be in charge, with no older brother or parents to boss me around.

"Okay, let's go!" Dave exclaimed. We paid our admission to a bored senior citizen at the main gate and started to prowl.

We looked at the rides first, the Roundup and Scrambler being the wildest of them all as usual. The freak show would be a must, the allure of the Half Man, Turtle Boy, and the woman who drove a spike into her head was overpowering to young boys.

"Let's go in now," Dave insisted. "Look, a show's starting now."

Even I couldn't resist. "Okay, let's go with it," I agreed. We paid a dime each and entered through a grimy tent flap into the inner sanctum.

"Oh wow," Dave said. Sitting on a pedestal was a young man with no legs. He wore a shirt that hung straight down and was rounded at the bottom, making him appear cut off at the belly button instead of the hips.

A carney barker stood with a microphone, shouting needlessly at the thin crowd of gawkers. "Here he is, ladies and gentlemen," even though the audience was all male, "the Half Man. Cut in two by an accident during a magician's act. He

survives only by a miracle of modern medicine."
The half man stared back at us, bored but unable
to escape. He folded his arms across his chest and
yawned. The barker flung an arm at the man with
a flourish, waiting for the applause which never
came. He finally gave up and pulled a cord which
dropped a curtain in front of the man.

"Now welcome Turtle Boy." The curtain arose
on a small man whose arms were missing at the
elbows and legs at the knees. "Born to a man of
the sea, this phenomenon was caused by a diet
too heavy in sea food." Someone laughed and the
carney barker glared for a moment before continuing. "Turtle Boy has learned to exist in a world of
normal people as best he can. Although he speaks
no known language, he communicates with dol-
phins and other sea creatures with a high pitched
squeak."

On cue, Turtle Boy threw back his head and
screeched a long, loud noise. He shuffled forward
on his stubs to a pack of cigarettes and a Zippo
lighter. Painstakingly he shook a filterless Phillip
Morris Commander from the package with his
mouth and picked it up with his lips. He flicked
the lighter open with his elbows and rolled the
striker over the flint. A flame popped up on his
first try and he lit the cigarette. This brought a
small burst of applause from the crowd and Turtle Boy nodded his head with no expression.

Enchatra was next, a woman who pounded nails
which looked like rubber into her head. Her hair
was long and thick, serving well as a prop to hide
the way she did the trick. Electro Boy was also very
much a fake, but his presentation was better as
electricity seemed to shoot from his fingers.

We exited the freak show amazed at the number
of odd people there were in the world. Actually,

when we looked around the fairgrounds it was not such a wonder after all. County fairs are by no means huge, so it took less that an hour for us to check out everything. We ended in a far corner near a John Deere display, where I was admiring the latest combine with stereo and air-conditioned enclosed cab. I was bemoaning the sorry state of our modern farmer who couldn't take the heat, noise, and dust when Dave grabbed my arm and put a finger to his lips.

I heard it immediately, low and menacing voices seeming to come from a large John Deere tractor at the far side of the display. We looked around, noticing that there was no one else in this remote display area. We tiptoed toward the sounds, like two hunters tracking a prey. Peering over a wagon, we could see five boys not much older than ourselves standing over a teenager sprawled on the ground at their feet. The five looked like thugs, or hoods as we called them, with greased back hair in duck tails at the back. They all wore jeans and white tee shirts with pockets. Cigarette packs bulged in the pocket of two, while the other three rolled them in their sleeves.

"We want it all now," growled one boy, a Camel hanging from his mouth like a lit piece of chalk. I could smell his Brylcream from where I stood.

"I gave it to you already," groaned the boy on the ground. His nose and mouth were smeared with blood.

"You've got to have more than three bucks," another boy threatened. He held a stick in his hand that looked like a long tent peg and he hit the boy on the ground hard, just below his left knee.

A small scream of pain escaped through his clenched teeth and he rolled into a ball, a woolly worm trying to feel protected. "I don't have any more," he moaned, the fear in his voice almost a physical thing.

"What do we do?" Dave hissed at me. "I think maybe they're going to kill that kid."

"I know." I looked again and the gang started moving closer to their victim. "We've got to show ourselves to draw them away from him."

"What should we do, fight them?" Dave asked, ready to take on a challenge.

"No. We stand up, yell, then run like the devil is after us. Those aren't kids having a friendly neighborhood fight. These guys are mean and we're out of their league."

"Okay," he agreed. "You go to the left and I'll go to the right. We'll make them split up."

"Good idea," I said. "Well, let's do it."

"Stop, oh please stop," the boy on the ground begged, and at that we stepped out from behind the wagon. They were about to start the beating in earnest, and the boy rolled into an even tighter ball.

"Hey you snot brains," I bellowed at the top of my lungs. Snot brains? Well, it just came out. I got the desired reaction at least, because the kicking stopped and all eyes turned to me. "You can kick each other when you get to reform school," I continued, at last saying something that made sense.

Everyone just stared. Seconds ticked by like minutes, and we just stood there like time had ceased to move. Even the human woolly worm lifted his head and looked at me. I thought we would stay like this until the fair closed two weeks later, and be carried away by the John Deere dealer like props in an advertising display. Dave finally got action. He spat in the general direction of the gang, not even coming close. No words, no taunts or threats, just a thimble full of spit. With a roar they leapt as one, rushing toward us with cat-like speed.

I kind of yelped and bolted to my left, as planned, and promptly tripped over the tongue of the wagon. They were on me like scum on a pond. Fists, feet, teeth, everything came at me as I kicked and hit blindly in all directions. There were so many of them that it was not hard to find a target. Flailing away, I felt and heard the crunch of gristle as a nose went flat under the knuckles of my right hand. My left fist was cut from someone's front teeth, and my foot landed fairly securely into a crotch.

Despite my punches, they were pounding on me with a vengeance. Blood was in my eyes and I tasted it salty in my mouth. I went back to the ground from their onslaught, and suddenly I was not being attacked any more. Groggily I looked up and saw Dave pounding one hoodlum and the bloody face of the boy we had helped came into view, holding two others around the neck. One of the thugs was running away, and the last stood by, obviously trying to decide what to do. His hesitation was his undoing, as I reached out and grabbed his ankle. With a hard pull he went to the ground and I rolled on top of him, hitting him at least a dozen times before I jumped up to help my comrades.

It was all over. The three thugs that Dave and the stranger had handled were running in the same general direction as the first deserter. The boy whom I had just released scrambled to his feet, gave us the universal sign of contempt, and ran after them. He was bawling like a newly branded calf.

We were all a mess. Swelling lips and eyes, blood from scrapes and cuts, and dark bruises were already forming. It was dreadfully quiet in the aftermath of the fighting, but we stood silently for a time, catching our breath, and feeling the pain.

At last the young man broke the silence. "Name's Al Stockton. I reckon you two are Gabriel one and two." He gave us a lopsided grin because his lips were swelling on the left side of his face.

"Gabriel?" Dave asked.

"Y'all must be, because I was one dead duck unless I got help from some angels, and there you were." He laughed heartily, then turned his head and spit blood.

"Well, our names here on earth are Dave and Bill," I answered, pointing to each of us in turn. "We just happened to be here, and could tell you were in pretty deep trouble."

"You were shore right," he drawled. "I got to tell you those punks had me, they did." He shook his head in shame, as if it were wrong to be beaten by a crowd.

"We really didn't plan on fighting them," I admitted. "Our plan was to get them to chase us and let you go. Besides, they had all of your money."

Al grinned again, wincing this time as the swelling had increased. "Like fun they did." He unbuckled his belt and pulled it with a whisk from his faded blue jeans. He opened a zipper hidden behind leather folds and revealed the tips of folded twenty dollar bills. He pulled two from the cramped compartment, and it appeared that there were many more.

"Holy smoke," Dave gasped, his swollen eyes opening wide in spite of himself.

"I'd never want to see th' day when a bunch of wet behind the ears street scum could get my money. My daddy taught me better'n that." He zipped the compartment shut and it disappeared under the folds of leather.

"But they could have killed you," I protested.

"Would have for pretty much sure if I had given this up," he said. "A thousand bucks would have put them on top of the world ya' know."

"A thousand bucks," Dave repeated in awe. "You brought a thousand dollars to the Allen County Fair?"

"Well, I pretty much had to if I was to buy this year's champeen hog," he declared. "Last year the old boy went for seven hundred beans, and this year I mean to have 'im."

"You must be a farmer," I said.

"Yep. At least ways I am now. I come out here from Oklahoma to take over my uncle's place. He died and left me a house, a barn full of really old equipment, and eight hundred acres."

"Wow," I replied. "That's a great gift."

"Don't 'ah know it. Ah figure if ah stock it with some prime animals, 'ah kin end up as one barn burner of a farmer." He waved his hands in the air for emphasis, the two twenty dollar bills in his left hand flapping in the breeze.

"I didn't think when we first saw you that you were any older than us," I said.

"Shoot, 'ah turned nineteen on March sixteen," he answered. "Always did have a baby face. Course, that don't hurt none with the girls does it?"

"I guess not," I said, a bit embarrassed. "Well, are you all right?" I inquired.

"Yeah, fine. Jest fine. How about y'all?" he asked, including us both with a nod of his head.

"Fine, I think," said Dave. "You and Bill got the worst of it."

"Well, I'm okay," I added. "I feel like I went ten rounds with Joe Lewis, but I'm all right." My fingers were gently exploring my cracked and swollen face. "I think I'll live."

"Well," Al declared, "here's a little somethin' to make the rest of your day at the fair more fun." He held out a twenty dollar bill to each of us, the pleasure showing in his eyes at our astonished looks.

"We didn't help you for money," I protested. "You were just a guy in trouble."

Neither of us reached for the money. Al stepped forward and pressed it into our hands. "Ya take it," he insisted. "Good deeds need a reward." He turned on his heel and started walking away. "Thanks again, angels," he tossed over his shoulder.

"Thank you, Al," Dave shouted, a huge grin covering his face.

"Good luck with that pig," I added. He waved into the air without turning around.

Dave and I studied the money in our hands, crinkling it and feeling the smooth texture. We were at a loss as to what we should do, the events of the past few minutes more numbing than exciting. "What do we do now?" I finally asked.

Dave grinned, waving his money in the air. "We spend it, stupid," he cried, pulling me by the arm to get me moving. "Let's eat sausage and onion sandwiches till we bust."

The rest of the day was a bit of a blur, consisting of food, video games, countless numbers of skill games which heavily favored the carneys, and almost every ride on the midway. We ended the day with two stuffed toy clothes pins, one small Bugs Bunny plastic blow up figure, and two teddy bears. Oh, and of course, we each had a nasty belly ache. Fortunately Dave's brother had not left us, but he was pretty angry that we kept him waiting for almost an hour. He was even less civil when, on our way home, Dave threw up in the back seat of his car.

"Don't ever ask me to take you anywhere again," he shouted at me as he sped away from the corner of Bluelick and Kool roads. He was so angry he refused to go one bit out of his way so that I could be dropped off at home.

I didn't really care, because I had the opportunity to walk off a bit of the fair food. Tossing my bear into the air as I walked, I thought about that day. Life was truly a matter of change, events, and opportunities landing in our paths almost at random. We happened to be there to help someone who could have been killed, and I guess maybe you could say I helped save a life. Chance and happenstance. A car happens to be on the same highway as a drunk driver. The drunk chooses that exact moment to pass out and swerve into the path of that car. A tiny cancer cell happens to survive the onslaught of millions of white corpuscles, living to grow and multiply and spread. Accidents. Freaks of nature. Happenstance. Or could it be the plan of our life.

Chapter 21

The Three Stooges were coming to the Ohio Theatre. Not just a movie or some of their popular short comedies, but the actual Stooges themselves. I was in a panic, afraid that my mother would not get me to the box office in time to buy one of the fifty cent tickets which would assure my seat. Rick did not want to go, considering the trio a silly, childish act for immature audiences. That was fine with me, because now I would have just one less person to worry about buying the last ticket.

My heart sank as we approached the downtown theatre. A huge line awaited the opening of the ticket office, which was nearly an hour away. I kept my silence, however, because I had won a heated argument with my parents just to be permitted to go to the performance. Many adults disliked the two Howard brothers and their companion Larry Fine. They poked each others eyes, pounded fingers and heads with a hammer, and started food fights. Some "'experts," mostly those trying to sell a book, claimed that the Stooges promoted violence and encouraged children to hurt each other. The Stooges decided to go on tour, their purpose being to warn youngsters that it was just an act. Of course, kids flocked to see their favorite clowns, but not to hear the message that almost all of them understood anyway.

"Now be careful and don't talk to strange men," my mother warned as I jumped from the car.

"Yes, Mother." I had never encountered one of those strange people that lurked in the shadows, but she always had me searching for them.

"I'll pick you up on North Street, as close to the door as I can," she continued nervously.

"Okay," I said cheerily, knowing that until I got to the back of that line I was still vulnerable to being stopped. My father had cast the deciding vote in allowing me to attend, saying "Oh, let the boy go. He knows better than to try the stuff those Stooges do." But he wasn't with us, which meant his decision could be vetoed. I was also fortunate in the fact that they hadn't gotten any telephone calls from parents of my Sunday school classmates who I had plinked in the eyes or bopped in the head with a "Nuk, nuk, nuk."

"You're going to be careful, aren't you?" my mother asked suspiciously, keeping me a captive at the car as the ticket line grew like a snake swallowing a pig.

"Of course I will," I said, fighting to keep the edge from my voice. "The line's getting longer, Mom."

"I don't care about that line," she snapped. "I want to know you're going to be very careful and promise me that you're not going to run around poking people in the eyes after this thing."

"No, of course not," I said as innocently as possible. "That stuff is dangerous you know." I was attempting to give her my Bambi look.

"Well, I just want you to know that I'm against this," she reminded me, frowning as she refused to permit my escape. "Your father is too easy on you boys," she lamented, and the ticket line grew even larger.

"Thanks for saying yes, Mom" I said, and then played my trump card. I kissed her on the cheek.

She blushed and waved her hand, looking like a schoolgirl who was unexpectedly kissed by her date. I was free.

"Oh, go on," she said, and I flew from the car like Superman flinging himself from a telephone booth. I sprinted toward the end of that dreadful line, my lungs bursting from the effort as I saw four, then seven, now ten more kids reach the line before me.

A harried looking Ohio Theater employee came by, handing out numbers in an attempt to keep some semblance of order. My number was nine hundred eighty four. "How many seats?" I asked him as I grabbed the precious plastic disc.

"One thousand," he said, moving on by as he spoke. "Hang on to that number, because you don't get in without it."

I stuffed it into my pocket and heard the wails of anger as, sixteen people later, the last plastic treasure was handed out. Immediately the kids with no number started working the line, offering as much as ten dollars for a number. I looked at my feet, not wanting to even make eye contact with the less fortunate, fearing they would key on me like a beggar asking for a handout.

Eternity clicked by, one slow motion second at a time, until finally the line began to move. I had seen freight trains starting forward from a dead stop move faster than this line. A second line formed, pleading, arguing, and even threatening those of us with a number. One girl, sensing that the hand buried in my pants pocket clung to the plastic treasure, tried to pull it out like a stopper in a drain.

"Get you hands off me," I snapped like a dog protecting its bone, and pulled my arm away with a wench of my hips, the right hand staying nestled in the protection of my pocket. Without hesitation the girl moved along to another person in the line.

Several police officers soon appeared, concerned perhaps that a riot could break out. The line ground slowly on, the front door of the Ohio Theater gobbling patrons one by one like a hungry man eating peanuts. Each moment brought me closer to trading my plastic disc for an admission ticket.

"Ladies and gentlemen." A bald man in a cheap suit two sizes too small stood with a borrowed police bullhorn. He wore a gold name badge that said S. Sandman, Manager. Getting no attention from either line he tried again. "Ladies, Gentleman, Children." That worked, and the two lines of faces, one eager and one disappointed, looked in his direction for at least a moment. Mr. Sandman used the moment and quickly continued, "Due to your tremendous response, the Three Stooges have agreed to a second show." The have-not line erupted in joy, the have line sighed with relief. Some who had paid ten dollars for a fifty cent ticket cursed. "Please get in line behind the last person with a number, and we will reissue numbers after everyone has been seated for the first show."

A stampede erupted, people pushing and running for a spot in line. I held my ground and pushed away several kids who were trying to push in front of me. It was over in less that a minute. One long line again stood where once there were two. Several people who had pushed into the line were ordered back to the end by stern policemen who were watching everything that was going on. Finally, after what seemed like an eternity, I reached the ticket window and was in.

I had brought two dollars with me. Fifty cents was gone for the ticket, and I had planned on popcorn and a traditional Ohio Theatre flat, tasteless fountain cola. Then I saw the promotional items and was hooked like a big trout. There were Three Stooges pencils for a quarter. A plastic cup went for seventy five cents. Tee shirts were two dollars and hung tantalizingly from metal hangers hooked over the back of the wall. A special display with a hand-lettered sign said "AUTOGRAPHED". Three illegible signatures that could have been anything were scrawled below each Stooge's picture. These went for a whopping twelve dollars.

My stomach soon forgotten, I soon owned a plastic cup, two pins, and a pencil. I also discovered that someone made a mistake, fortunately in my favor, and sold the tickets in reverse order. In other words, the person who purchased the first ticket got the last seat in the theater, moving forward until the front row was sold to the last numbers.

So here I was, graven images in my head and on my shirt, perched proudly in the center of the first row. Truly, this must be heaven.

Of course, an awful lot of arguing and shouting was going on from the people who had waited for several hours in the front of the line, but nothing could be done. No one was going to voluntarily give up his seat in the front for a place in the rear. The only thing that could solve the problem finally happened. The Three Stooges walked onto the stage.

Of course, the theater erupted. My ears hurt from the din but I took the pain like a man and looked carefully at the Stooges one by one. I was amazed at how old they looked, suddenly realizing that they were not at all like the characters I saw on the television screen. They were mortal men and looked tired. They smiled and waved at the screaming mob of kids, patiently waiting for the noise to abate.

Finally Moe was able to speak. "Quite a crowd, eh boys?"

"Yeah," declared Larry.

"Soitanly," added Curly, including his famous "Nuk, nuk, nuk." The crowd went wild again

The Stooges talked to us like we were all old friends. They didn't hit each other or poke eyes. They just explained that what we saw in their films was just pretend, an act they perform for their fans. I watched them carefully, not missing a movement. Curly was sweating profusely from the bright lights and Moe's every wrinkle showed through his thick theater makeup. Larry looked smaller than I imagined and seemed content to let his companions do all of the talking.

They demonstrated in slow motion how their fingers don't really poke into each other's eyes, and even brought out hammers, pliers, and mallets made of soft rubber. All rather simple, direct, and well, boring. The kids were disappointed, and I think the Stooges felt bad, too. They were doing what someone was demanding they do. Their hearts were not a part of this activity. Maybe because we were all kids, or maybe because I could see it in their eyes from the front row. I discovered that instead of being in awe, I felt sorry for them.

Finally their presentation was over, like the end of a bad play. Applause grew again, forced from respect, not what we had just seen. When they reached the exit to my left I could still see them, even though they thought the black hanging curtains hid them from view. I saw their shoulders slump and the smiles fade. They became just three guys on the road, doing their job, and getting paid. They could have been building a bridge or laying brick, just three working stiffs. Then they disappeared into the darkness.

Several Stooge films were shown, funny and full of slapstick comedy as always. I laughed and enjoyed the antics then just as I do now, but something was gone. Maybe it was the magic of the unknown, the knowledge that my heroes had feet made of clay. When the last film ended and the house lights came on, the pitch men came down the aisles to sell memorabilia that made the serious money for the tour. I carefully placed my pins and pencil into the plastic cup and left them under my seat.

My mother took my quietness as excitement and was silent as we drove home. The line for the next show was excitedly moving into the theater.

Chapter 22

I find it interesting that although people lived some considerable distance from one another, there was still an abundance of communication that went on in a rural area. Men met at the Lafayette granary to sell corn, wheat, and soy beans or to have oats ground into feed for livestock. Their business typically took less than half of the time they were there, idle conversation and gossip filled the rest. I always begged to go along, not to help with the work but to play with the other youngsters.

My father was spending one such leisurely Saturday morning with a few farmers from Ada, a small town several miles from our farm. I immediately went exploring, the favorite preoccupation for all the kids that visited the granary. Remember, times were different then and we were country people, so we could do things that would have shocked most city people. For example, the boys always took their air rifles. The granary manager paid five cents for each dead rat and one penny for each dead mouse. Rodents were a plague to granaries, with thousands of pounds of valuable grain eaten each year, as well as the number of burlap bags destroyed by gnawing teeth. I considered our trips to be more like a safari, with the opportunity to bag big game.

I headed for the main storage area, where stacks of bagged chicken feed, goat chow, and every other Purina brand grain food in the universe was kept. Almost every sack on the bottom level had at least one hole eaten into it, and nests could usually be found almost anywhere. Industrious hunters could find dozens of rodents if they cared enough to move a lot of bags, or they could wait for them to come out into the open. I never moved the bags, not out of laziness but because of sport. I liked to perch on a high stack of bags and wait for a rat to belligerently stroll out in the open. Rats were tough and usually it took a pellet in the head to kill them. I've shot rats in the body and watched them just turn and stare at the spot where the BB went in. I was even once chased by an enraged rat who had no fear of people and did not appreciate the pain of my shooting it in the back side.

My air rifle slung over one shoulder, I felt like Chuck Conners in the *Rifleman* television series. I walked into the large building and inhaled the soft powdery scent of grain dust. Bright sun flowed through the windows, revealing so much of the dust in the air that it looked like liquid. I was a little disappointed that no other kids seemed to be around today, spoiling a perfect opportunity for socialization. Climbing a ten foot stack of burlap bags filled with cattle feed, I settled in with my back supported against a wide support beam. My legs hung over the top sack, dangling down like they were waiting for a foot stool. Within moments I saw a large rat, probably at least a pound, walk boldly across the open floor. Its belly was swollen from sweet grain and the rat was probably heading for its nest to nap away the afternoon.

I cocked my Daisy and levered a BB into the

chamber, aiming carefully at the rodent's head.
Just as I had been taught by my father I inhaled
deeply, let out half, then held my breath. Slowly I
squeezed the trigger until the spring released and
the BB shot forward. The rat leaped into the air,
landed on its back, kicked its feet ineffectually for
a moment, then lay still.

"Great shot." The praise came from my father
who had just walked in with five other men. They
nodded approvingly in agreement with him and
my cheeks burned with pride.

"This old boy won't steal feed any more," one
of the men said, kicking the dead rat into a corner.

"With an aim like that you'll be paying for college in no time," another added.

"Majoring in agriculture, of course," a third
added, looking at me with a smile.

"Yes, sir," I answered obligingly, proud of the
attention of the grown men.

"We're going to help John here load a pickup
with bags of feed," my father called up to me. "You
should see a lot of targets running around while
we're moving bags."

"Yeah, just don't aim at us," a big man wearing a bright red cap laughed. "My missus has told
me I'm a skunk before but never a rat."

We all laughed and I waved at him. "I won't
shoot you unless someone offers me a nickel to do
it," I said and everyone hooted.

"I'll give you a buck, kid," a skinny fellow in
baggy overalls hooted.

"Now, don't you guys start something I don't
want to see get finished," my father scolded good
naturedly.

"You know we're just kidding don't you, kid?"
the skinny fellow shouted.

"I know you're just kidding if you want me to shoot him for a buck" I answered. "Now, for five dollars...."

The men all howled with laughter again and slapped my father on the back. "I tell you, Kenny," the big man in the red hat bellowed, "that's an all-American boy you got there."

General hooting and laughing went on for a while until finally the men settled down to their work. Their activity brought out dozens of mice scurrying in fear as their homes were disturbed. I placed careful shot after shot into the little rodents, and soon they were piling up. The men kicked my bounty into a corner as I shot them, occasionally yelling encouragement.

Breaks were common as the men liked to visit much more than work, and the conversation got pretty lively at times. My father would raise an occasional eyebrow or shake his head, which helped prevent them from becoming too bawdy. Finally the truck was loaded and John headed for the pop machine to reward his help. He soon returned with frosty cold bottles of Dr. Pepper for each and handed an extra up to me. They settled down on sacks of feed below my perch and the conversation got serious.

"Did you fellows hear about the thief that's been prowling the township?" the man in the bib overalls asked. "He's been breaking in at night and stealing money and jewelry with people sleepin' right in their own beds."

"I not only heard about it," John said, "but my sister and her husband got a visit from the bas..., I mean from him. Sorry, kid." He grinned and waved his pop bottle up at me. I grinned and waved back.

"They actually had him in their house?" the

skinny fellow barked, leaning toward John in as-
tonishment.

"Yes, sir, they surely did," John said, warming
to the attention suddenly thrown his way. He
pushed his back against the sacks he was sitting
on and prepared to tell his story. "My brother-in-
law said he was dead to the world when somethin'
woke him. He lay real still, kind of spooked, you
know, wondering what bothered him. He smelled
perfume, real strong like it hurt his nose, you
know. It turned out the thief had knocked over a
bottle and it broke on the floor. That's probably
what woke him. He saw someone moving in the
room and thought it was my sister. He sat up in
bed and asked what was wrong. Well, the thief lit
out of there like the devil was on him."

"Did the sheriff get him?" my father asked.

"Naw, he was gone real quick. Probably went
into the corn field out back. You'd never catch him
there."

"This has been happening all over," one man
said. "A lot of people have taken to keeping guns
by the bed. Someone will take care of him in the
middle of the night and then we'll know who it is."

The conversation broke up soon after and I
gathered up my bounty. I made almost three dollars that day in the granary and saved a considerable amount of feed. I wondered about the thief,
who it could be, and why was he doing it, but of
course there was no answer that anyone knew.

That night I dreamed about an intruder. He
came into my room and was taking all of my pos-
sessions, my baseball cards, my pocket knife, my
fishing pole, everything that was important to me.
I yelled at him to stop, but he just laughed and
kept shoving things into his sack. I jumped out of
bed and ran to him, grabbing his thin shoulders

and spinning him around to face me. When he turned to me I saw his face. It was a bare white skull, grinning its sweet smile of death.

I awoke with a start, sweat running down my face and dampening my pillow. My heart was pounding in my ears and I had a violent need to go to the bathroom. After a moment I realized that I had been dreaming, and this was reality. My heart slowed to a dull thud and I lay still, trying to calm myself. Finally my full bladder warned me to get up or else, so I pushed up on my elbows.

Frozen in place like an ice sculpture and standing by my dresser was a dark figure. He was dressed in black but his head was bare. I could see his silhouette in my mirror, backlit by a half moon shining through my bedroom window. The figure must have known I was awake, because he still did not move. I didn't know if I should scream, cry, faint, or wet the bed like a two-year-old. I too froze in place, a rabbit in the thicket expecting camouflage and lack of movement to foil the hunter. I think we were staring at each other, although there was not enough light in the room to be sure. Someone had to do something. If the circumstances were not so serious this would seem silly.

My room filled with light with the suddenness of a bolt of lightening. My father stood in my doorway, his hand moving from the light switch to the trigger of his double barrel twelve gauge shotgun. Standing at my dresser, his mouth gaping open and his eyes riveted on the black opening of the barrels of the shotgun, was Bud Campbell.

My father tensed for an instant and then quickly pointed the shotgun toward the ceiling. He sank against the door jamb and looked at Bud with pain in his eyes. "Bud, you stupid fool," he said, more sad than angry. Bud started to cry. "Get to the kitchen," my father said, carefully easing the hammers down on the weapon. Clicking slightly as they moved reluctantly to a benign position, the shotgun seemed to resent not being permitted to discharge.

I scrambled wordlessly from bed and rushed to the bathroom, relieving myself noisily into the white porcelain oval filled with water. Rick was wide awake by now and sitting on a kitchen stool when I finally entered the room, and my mother sat worriedly next to him. Bud and my father both stood, my father leaning against the sink and Bud across the room, backside pushing into the edge of the stove. The shotgun was not in sight.

"Start talking, son," my father said flatly. His eyes bored into Bud like a cork screw.

"My father has been sick and hasn't worked for almost six months," Bud said, his eyes downcast and his voice low. "We don't have no food and the rent's not been paid for two months. My dad needs medicine that we can't buy and my mom cries all day. I tried to get full-time work but nobody will hire me because I'm too young and they know I'd have to quit school." He paused and rubbed his palms on pale white cheeks.

"I had to steal or we'd end up on the curb," he continued forlornly. "I know it's not right but I had to do something." His continence sank lower with each word and he seemed to physically shrink. If the oven door had been open he would have tumbled in like a hapless waif in Hansel and Gretel.

My mother dabbed at her eyes with a shredded facial tissue while Rick and I studied the top of the Formica-covered breakfast bar. Silence took over and filled the room like a suffocating cloak. Probably three minutes passed, although it felt like hours. At last my father turned and opened a drawer by the sink. He pulled a tablet and pen from within like a magician producing a rabbit from the top hat, and walked across the room to Bud. "Write down what you took and from whom. And I mean every last thing. I don't care if it was a thimble or a rusty nail."

Bud took the pad and started writing. Silence, driven away for a short time by my father, crept back like another thief and took over our house again. Occasionally the faint sound of the pen scratching over the pad could be heard and when Bud tore off a full sheet it sounded like a ship's sail being rent in two. At long last Bud finished and handed the pages to my father, who studied them with his head tilted back slightly to assist his bifocals.

He signed and lay the papers aside. "All right. Everyone back to bed. Bud, you come with me."

We did as we were told, no one saying another thing as we lay awake and listened to our car leave the driveway. I looked at my alarm clock and noted that it was four a.m.

My father was gone until seven that night. He came in the house looking worn and hungry. My mother had fixed meat loaf and warmed it quickly. We all sat quietly as my father ate his dinner and gathered his strength. Finally my mother asked "What did you do?"

He looked up and paused for a moment, as if he did not want to tell us. Finally he began. "Well, first we went to every person on the list. Thank goodness they were all home. If they could afford the loss I asked them to let it go. If they were poor I paid them for their losses. From the group that could financially handle the loss, only old John Johnson insisted he get his money, and he could buy and sell half the township."

"Did anyone want to press charges?" my mother asked.

"Not one. Old John wanted to but I told him if he called the police I wouldn't pay him for his loss, and of course he knew the Campbell's couldn't. His greed won out over his meanness."

"So no police," she said.

"No. And I went to see the pastor. He's going to help raise rent and food money until the Campbell's are back on their feet. Now if you'll excuse me" he said with a smile, "I'm going to bed. I feel like I've been through a war." He pushed up tiredly and headed toward much needed rest.

"What about the people who wanted their money?" I asked. "Who paid for their things?"

"Didn't you hear what your father said? He paid for those things," my mother said.

"Yeah, I know he gave them the money right at that moment, but where will the money come from to pay us back?"

"Your father paid for those things dear. He paid for them with no thought of getting the money back." She patted my hand and smiled.

"Can we afford that?" Rick asked.

"Of course not," my mother answered.

"Then why did he do it?" Rick asked.

"Because he's a good man." She said it simply and honestly.

"Then he kept Bud out of jail," I said.

"That's correct. What would it serve to ruin the life of a young man that was frightened and didn't know which way to turn. He's wrong, of course, because what he did could have gotten him or someone else killed."

"He didn't have a gun or anything," Rick interjected.

My mother smiled and shook her head. "Of course not. But what if someone woke up like your brother did and maybe had a heart attack from fear. Or what if your father had shot Bud last night?"

"He wouldn't have been at fault if he had shot Bud," I said in defense of my father. "Bud was robbing us."

"Would you like to ask your father to live his life and not be concerned that he killed Bud Campbell? Do you really think he could just forget about something like that?" She raised her eyebrows and waited for me to think about what she had just said.

"No, I guess not," I finally grudgingly replied.

She patted our hands and went into the refrigerator. Pulling out two bottles of grape juice, she handed each of us an icy treat. The humidity in the air condensed immediately on the clear glass and sweat ran down onto the kitchen counter. "Now, you boys have a cool drink and let me get this kitchen cleaned."

Rick retrieved a bottle opener from a drawer and opened his drink. He handed me the opener and I popped the cap from my bottle. I put the opener away and closed the drawer, then picked up both bottle caps. We drained the tart, yet sweet liquid in three gulps and left the kitchen. Rick to the basement to put the empty bottles away and I outside to play. When I pulled the door closed, I heard my mother singing softly as she cleaned the kitchen.

Chapter 23

Aunt Edie's condition was worsening. Sores came back on her legs and now spread to her arms. The maternity dresses were also being utilized again because her stomach had swollen to three times its normal size. A lot of whispering was going on in our home but few secrets were actually being kept. I asked Earl for a few days off work so I could be with her more. Instead of giving me a smart remark about taking all my time off when school started in a few weeks, he simply said I could take all of the time I needed. Even he seemed to know how little time she had.

Our walks were a thing of the past now, and she never came outside to score for me anymore when I played basketball. I began to feel uncomfortable around her, much to my shame, not knowing what to say or what I should do. She felt it too, even through the pain and all of the drugs.

"I'm getting worse every day, Billy," she said to me one morning. She looked so tired I wasn't sure that she could take another breath.

I didn't protest like usual, nor did I argue with her. The truth was too evident. "What can I do for you?" I asked, not knowing what else to say.

"How about singing to me?" she said, the twinkle of humor pushing through the pain in her eyes. She always liked to hear me sing and asked for a song whenever she could.

I waited for a few moments, expecting her to tell me what song to sing. After a bit I understood that she was waiting for me to begin. I wanted the song to be her choice, so I said "What would you like to hear?"

"*Amazing Grace,*" she said without hesitation. "Sing *Amazing Grace* for me Billy."

"I don't have the music to follow. I can sing as best I can from memory."

"Just do the best you can," she said quietly and closed her eyes. She was so frail. I wasn't sure that I could do this without her knowing I was crying.

I began to sing. "'Amazing Grace, how sweet the sound, to save a wretch like me. I once was lost, but now I'm found, was blind but now I see.'" She smiled as I continued the song, all signs of pain and stress gone from her face.

When I finished she sat quietly for a moment before opening her eyes slightly. "So, keep going," she said.

"It's over. That's the end of the song."

"I know that," she said, a bit angry it seemed. "Sing another song."

"Which one?" I asked.

"Don't make me keep choosing," she said. "Just pick a church hymn and sing."

I sang *Jesus Loves Me* and she smiled as I went on. I paused at the end, trying to decide which song should be next. She lay quietly, her hands folded over her chest in quiet repose. She looked so weak and frail, a bird dashed to the ground, bones too hollow to permit flight. Minutes passed and I became uncomfortable, itches attacking me under my arms and behind my knees. They were stabbing itches like needles sticking in my flesh, making me want to scratch and yell at the same time. Instead I sat still, not moving so much as a finger.

"Are you afraid?" Her voice, barely above a whisper, made me jump involuntarily.

I scratched my burning legs and armpits before I answered. "Yes, I guess I am."

She smiled a soft, easy grin, like a loving Mona Lisa. "You're an honest boy. There are some things you should never lose in life once you've found them." She paused for so long I thought she would not continue. A low, deep cough erupted from her throat, rattling through her chest like a loose chain. She squinted in pain and coughed hard again, squeezing her hands into balls with the effort. There were bright red drops of blood on her lips, like patches of cheap lipstick. "Always tell the truth," she finally finished.

"Yes, ma'am" I answered.

Aunt Edie opened one eye with a great effort and trained it on my face. "You're blurred," she said

"I was always a bit out of focus," I answered, wiping away the tears.

She smiled and then chuckled a bit, the laughter causing another bout of coughing. Her hands gripped the thin blanket that covered her and I heard the fabric give away with a loud rip. Blood sprayed in a fine mist as she coughed again, dotting her cheeks and my shirt like tiny freckles. "I want to tell you something," she gasped. When I didn't respond she said "Are you listening to me?"

"Yes, oh yes I am," I hurriedly said.

"Good. I want you to know something else." She raised a hand and I took it gently in mine.

"What is it?" I asked, leaning closer to her so I could hear. As her breath labored I could smell the sickening sweet scent of decaying flesh.

"Don't be afraid. There is not one thing in this world that can hurt you for more than a very short time." She gripped my hand harder, her nails cutting into my flesh. I did not flinch or move a single muscle. "Nothing that happens can be changed because we want it to be. Instead of worrying about what will happen, just attack life and use it. Fear is a waste of time. The only way we can stop existing is when no one cares anymore. If you remember me, I'll always be near." She opened both her eyes now, wide and round as if that would help her to see more clearly. "Do you understand?" she almost shouted.

"Yeah, I understand," I said, the tears dripping on her hands now pressed to my lips. "I won't be afraid, and I won't forget you, I promise."

She sank back on her pillow, relief showing on her pale face. Her eyes closed again and she renewed her strength. Only her hand did not relax as she held onto me tightly. After a few minutes she breathed deeply and spoke again. "Would you please get your mother for me" she said.

"Sure. I'll be just a second" I said. My legs felt like wooden pegs as I ran outside to find my mother. She was hanging fresh laundry on the line, a stiff breeze fighting to control a queen size sheet she was adjusting on the line. She smiled at me as I ran toward her, looking tired from the strain she had been under. "Aunt Edie needs you now," I blurted. "You need to come quick."

My mother instantly ran for the house, throwing a handful of clothes pins into the grass. I was on her heels, reaching around her to open the back door. The wind, as if surprised by her lack of attention, grabbed the unattended sheet and lifted it from the clothes line. It gusted under the outstretched broad cotton fabric and turned it into a sail. The sheet flew like magic over the fence and into the chicken yard. The damp fabric clung to the dusty ground, and the chickens came running in anticipation of something to eat. They scratched at the sheet, pecking for the food that wasn't there.

My mother and I ran into the house without glancing back. Aunt Edie was motionless and looked like she was asleep. "Edith," my mother said breathlessly.

"Hi," she said, almost drunk from the morphine that was helping to control her pain. "I need you to do something for me, Waneta."

"Of course. What is it?" my mother asked.

"Call an ambulance please. I'm afraid it's my time," Aunt Edie said softly. A trickle of blood now ran from the corner of her mouth. "But call Eddie first," she said and smiled fondly at the sound of his name.

The scene that was played when Aunt Edie came to us was now repeated in reverse. The ambulance crew came and banged their way into our living room with all of their equipment. They loaded her onto the gurney like expert movers transporting valuable art work. She was so frail and light there was no effort in moving her. They went about their business quietly, respecting our grief as they prepared to take her for the last time. Only an occasional moan from Aunt Edie showed us that there was still life in her wispy shell.

My mother rode in the ambulance as it rolled away quickly, no sirens demanding the right of way, but the ever present lights clicked left and then right. Rick and I were ordered to stay at home in case anyone should call. My father was on his

way to the hospital and Uncle Eddie had left his
mother's house, which was near the hospital.

They whisked her away like someone cleaning
up after a party, everyone knew what had happened but the evidence was gone. I sat on her hospital bed in the living room just to hold onto the
tangible feeling of her presence. There was such
an eerie silence in the house I felt like I was in a
vacuum. Sunlight streamed through the picture
window in the front of the house and covered the
bed like a spotlight. I looked at Aunt Edie's pillow
and saw the red stains on the stark white pillow-
case. They were already dried and becoming a dark
brown as I looked at them. That was the moment
I knew it was over. I began to sob.

Chapter 24

My parents came home after dark, my mother red-eyed and shaking, holding on to my father's arm. I was sitting by the fireplace in our living room, not wanting to be very far away from the last place I had seen Aunt Edie. I also had brought Daisy in the house with me for comfort, a major infraction of the rules of our home. She sat quietly panting as I stroked her head and did not bound to her feet when the door opened. She looked at my parents and thumped her tail in greeting, but did not move from my side.

After helping my mother to their bedroom my father went to the basement where Rick had escaped with a book. I heard their voices but could not discern what was said. My father's shoes made a slow clumping sound on the wooden stairs as he trudged slowly up to the kitchen. He paused for a moment as if to collect his thoughts before coming to me. He looked dreadfully tired and sad. My heart ached for him and for what I knew he had to say.

"You know how sick your Aunt Edie is, don't you, Son?"

"Yes. She was in a lot of pain, too," I replied. I twisted my hands together to keep them from shaking.

He nodded and walked slowly to a high backed chair at the right of the fireplace hearth and sank heavily into the cushions. "The doctor told us she had cancer spreading all through her body," he continued. "They did all they were able to do for her, at least all that we know how to do."

Tears slid down my cheeks like rain rolling over a windshield. "She died, didn't she?" I said, a statement more than a question.

His answer was spoken so softly I almost didn't hear his actual reply. "Yes. She passed away about two hours ago."

"It isn't fair," I sobbed, attempting to replace my grief with anger. "She didn't do anything wrong. She never hurt anybody." I suddenly started feeling sick and thought I would make a mess on the living room carpet, but somehow I didn't care.

"Of course it isn't fair," my father said. "You're too young to understand that, but there's nothing that can be done. Just try to remember her as she was before she got sick. She's like that again, only even better now."

I didn't answer, not because I didn't believe in heaven, but because I was angry and sad that Aunt Edie had to go there now.

"What are you thinking?" my father asked me after we sat in silence for a few minutes.

"I'm thinking she said she wasn't afraid," I said. "Only I don't believe it. I think she told me she wasn't afraid so I would be brave."

He nodded his head slowly in agreement. "I don't think anyone would be normal if they weren't afraid when death came. That's the way we're made, Son. The will to live is something God gave us to emphasize the value of life. You should also be proud that even though she was dealing with a situation that severe, her thought was to comfort you."

He stood and walked over to me, resting a work worn hand on my bowed head. "Your aunt lived a life of pride and dignity, Bill. She died the same way. If we could all handle ourselves on this earth the same way, heaven would be a very crowded place." He patted me gently and left the room.

Chapter 25

The Stoners and Kellers would never use the service of any funeral director except Chiles and Sons in downtown Lima. I learned that Aunt Edie had arranged everything quite some time ago, from the style of her casket to the type of vault that would protect her remains. Even the payment for the service was taken care of in advance. She had told my mother that it was too traumatic after someone was gone to ask the family to pick out something sensible. She knew Uncle Eddie would buy the most expensive of everything, and she would not have that. Of course, he upgraded everything before the arrangements were complete.

I decided that funerals were beyond any doubt the most disgusting, barbaric display that was known to man. Several showings each day were held to allow family and friends to pay proper respect. Each session started with appropriate solemnity. I expected a lot of grief and compassion, but as the crowd grew, so did the level of noise. People talked and visited like they were attending a family reunion, which I guess in a way they were. Cousins, friends, coworkers, all came to say goodbye. The visiting slowly increased until there was lots of laughing and general frivolity. I finally left the chapel and went exploring.

Two other smaller rooms, or chapels as they were called by the funeral home, held a body also. Elvira Matthews lay in rest with only four small arrangements of fresh flowers keeping her company. Her casket was very plain and, I suspected, not very expensive. Elvira was old, probably around eighty I would guess, and had that look of a person who lived hard and seldom saw much happiness.

I wandered over to the small stand that held a guest register and noted that only nine lines were written in with names. Walking back to the casket, I searched the lined face for something, although I didn't know what. Where was her family? Her friends? It didn't seem very fair.

Padding along the rose patterned carpet, I returned to Aunt Edie's room. It was packed with people, all seeming to be talking at the same time. I approached her casket from the foot, not wanting to draw attention, because I wanted a private visit. She looked so peaceful dressed in a light blue silk dress that was her favorite. The pain that became a daily visitor and showed itself to the outside world around her mouth and the corners of her eyes was gone. I realized that I hadn't seen my real Aunt Edie for a long time. The cancer had consumed her, leaving no room for anything else. Looking at her now, I realized that as terrible as we all felt that she was gone, those feelings were selfish. She could not have wanted to linger in that condition.

"Aunt Edie," I whispered. "There's a little old lady over in the other room that doesn't have much. Would you mind if we shared with her?" I knew what she would say if she could. I reached out to pat her and then couldn't do it. I didn't want to remember the icy cold touch. She was warm and alive in my heart, so I determined to keep her that way for my memories.

No one paid the least bit of attention to me as I headed toward the exit once again. Without breaking stride I slid a small planter with several green and yellow plants into my hands and held it in front of me as I headed toward Elvira Matthew's chapel. Plucking the card off the plastic stem that held it above the foliage, I read "With sympathy, John and Nora Walker." I stuck the card in my pocket and walked to a window sill near Elvira's casket. With the planter secured in its place, I felt better and left her to rest alone. I hoped that someone would take the plants home and keep them alive for years, remembering Elvira when they watered them.

Three days went by quickly, the morning of the third meaning preparation for the burial service. The hospital bed and all of the medicines were gone from our home. Uncle Eddie stayed with his mother in Lima, so we felt for the first time in a long time what it was like to be just the four of us together. It is strange how quickly we get used to things. The house felt empty without Aunt Edie there with us. We were all quiet as we finished breakfast and prepared to go to the funeral home. The only real unanswered question at the time was Rick's behavior. He came home after each funeral home visitation, changed his clothes, and left the house without a word. He came back just in time to get ready for the next showing. He was always covered with grime and sweat and had to shower before we could leave. My parents would murmur in feigned secrecy while he went to the shower.

Uncle Eddie came by that morning, drawing our concern from Rick for at least a moment. Tears brimming in his eyes, Uncle Eddie traded hugs with my mother and father. "Come with me," he said and herded us like ducks out the door.

"What is it, Eddie?" my mother asked, moving despite having no answer. Daisy was running around us by now, barking and jumping as best she could on her three legs.

"You've got to see this," he said again, gesturing for us to get in his car. He looked excited, and yet fatigue and sorrow darkened his eyes. The last few months had turned him into an old man.

"I went home to pick up some things," he said as his big Mercury backed down our driveway. "I haven't been there since Edie...well, you know," he said, unable to say she died. "I don't want to go there anyway without her, but I needed to do some things." He rounded the corner at Bluelick Road, giving the stop sign little more than a cursory glance.

My mother, sunk into the thick leather padding in the back seat, pushed forward until she was perched on the edge of the seat, and leaned over her brother-in-law's shoulder. She spoke so softly I could barely hear. "Eddie, what happened. Did you see something terrible at home?"

"Oh, no," he said, too emotional to speak quietly. "This is wonderful."

My mother sank back into her seat, giving my father a quizzical look. He raised his eyebrows and shrugged slightly. Rick and I sat in front with Uncle Eddie. I tried to catch Rick's attention but he was studying his hands in his lap, picking at some dirt under his fingernails. We sped along at a high rate of speed, the big Mercury humming along effortlessly.

My mother's childhood home jumped into view, a huge brick farm house built to last forever. Across the street sat my parent's first home, built of wood purchased from the Lima tank plant. Huge pallets brought in parts to assemble Army tanks, which were sold for a quarter or fifty cents each. My mother used to say she pulled out nails all day long while my father was at work, then he took the two by fours one board at a time and pounded the nails back in. The end result was a small home that they lived in for ten years.

Another stop sign was ignored as Uncle Eddie turned to travel the last three hundred yards to his home. He slowed down at the spot where our family dog of many years ago was once hit by a car. I remembered little of that dog, except her name was Nipper, she was harmless, and there was a great deal of blood when she was hit.

The car swung into his drive, the crumbling blacktop surface showing blotchy black and white, needing a coat of sealer. He stopped the car by the garage, which positioned us at the side of the house. The layout of their house was identical to ours, another sign of the closeness of the relationship between Aunt Edie and Mother. "Come with me," Uncle Eddie urged, and he led us to the back of the house. He stopped for a moment to rub new tears from his eyes, then pointed a finger to Aunt Edie's precious flower garden.

Every weed was gone, a condition which was almost never seen before. Not only were the weeds gone, but the earth was carefully tilled around each plant, even to the point of the dirt being smoothed around each stem. Not a pebble was to be found in the garden, plus the soil was dark and rich from the addition of peat to hold moisture. Each flower stood tall and proud, like individual soldiers dressed for a parade. Even the edge of the flower garden was trimmed and cut out with razor perfect precision. Some of the weaker plants were gently staked with dark green sticks, enabling them to add to the beauty of the garden.

"Look," Uncle Eddie sniffed, blowing his nose noisily with a handkerchief that appeared from his pocket.

"Wow," I exclaimed, marveling with a nurseryman's eye how glorious it looked when the job was completed. Aunt Edie had always known how it could look, which was why she kept at us to finish the job. We never had the gumption to make it look like this, nor she the drill sergeant personality to force us. Now I wished she could have seen it while she was alive.

"Who did this?" my mother asked. She looked from one of us to another with wide-eyed wonder. "She never had this garden so beautiful when she did it all herself. She always said she just didn't have the time."

My father thrust his hands into his pockets and rocked back and forth from heel to toe. He nodded his head approvingly. "This is a wonderful tribute," he declared. Hands still buried in his pockets, he walked the length of the exhibit, stopping and bending over occasionally to examine a plant or to look at the precise edge cut into the ground to form the perfect border. After making his inspection, he strolled back to us, still nodding his head, "Very nice work. Now," he paused and removed his left hand from hid pants pocket and raised a closed fist with an extended index finger into the air, "who do you suppose might have done this wonderful thing."

He walked over to Rick, who stood with his head down. I saw tears drip one by one from his nose and land on his freshly shined shoes. My father placed a hand on his eldest son's shoulder, reaching up because Rick was a full five inches taller. "Could this have been done by someone who mysteriously disappeared for hours on end these last few days? Someone who didn't want to make a big deal out of what he was doing, and just wanted to take care of the job on his own?"

Rick lifted his eyes and they locked onto mine. "We should have finished this a long time ago. She paid us time and again with tickets, food, money, anything we wanted. Well, we just should have finished, that's all."

My father pulled him close and they hugged. "You did well son. You did very, very well," he said.

We all stood for a moment looking at the garden before reluctantly walking back to the car. Uncle Eddie patted Rick on the back and my mother put her arm around him as they walked. I brought up the rear, smiling within myself. I learned that day just a little but more what being a man is all about. I was proud of my brother.

We arrived at the funeral home around twelve thirty. The service was scheduled for one thirty. Without a chapel full of family and friends, we had little to do or say as we waited. Uncle Eddie stood at the casket for most of the hour, not wanting to say good-bye to the woman he loved for so many years. My mother sat staring at the casket, looking tired and drawn. My father stayed at her side, patting her hand and whispering to her occasionally with words of comfort.

I went to a small room that contained two sofas, five straight backed chairs, a coffee pot, and a snack machine. Rick was there, eating a candy bar. I walked over to the sofa where he sat looking totally dejected. Swinging a chair around in front of him, I sat on it backwards, hanging my arms over the back of the chair and resting my chin on the padded top. He looked up at me and raised his eyebrows in an unasked question.

"How's it going?" I asked, trying to be brilliant and say something profound.

"I didn't do that so anyone would make a big deal over it," he said as if I had asked the question that was in my mind. "I finished that garden for Aunt Edie."

"I know that," I said, my head bobbing up and down as I talked, because my chin was resting on the back of the chair.

"I can't believe we didn't finish that while she was still alive, Billy," he said. "She should have been able to see it."

"You know, Rick," I said, lifting my head to make it easier to talk, "somehow I think she not only can see it but probably watched as you finished the work."

He looked at his half-eaten candy bar for a moment and held it out to me. I shook my head so he shoved it in his mouth. He chewed for a couple of minutes before speaking again. "You know, it may seem weird, but I could have sworn a couple of times I heard her say 'Richard, that's a weed over there not a flower. And do you call that soil smoothed and level?' That made me do a better job."

"It certainly is beautiful," I said with sincerity.

"Yeah, it does look pretty good, I guess," he admitted. "I'm sure she at least would grade me a B for it."

I smiled at the thought of her critical eye. "I doubt anyone could ever get an A when it came to her garden. She was tough."

"Yeah," he smiled back, "but that's why we'll do okay with anyone else, as long as we work up to Aunt Edie's standards."

We sat silently for a while, not really needing to say more. Finally I glanced at the clock and saw that it was time. "We'd better get in there" I said, "It's time to tell her good-bye."

EPILOGUE

She was buried in a large cemetery with many others who have left this life. I felt sure she was happy with that, because she liked to be around others. I remember her telling my mother that she didn't like being alone because it seemed like such a waste of time.

The service was quite nice, with lots of songs that she loved and people there who remembered and cared for her. I'm not really sure why I felt the way I did, but I didn't cry. Maybe I was cried out, or maybe I thought I should be strong and help my mother. I know I saved my tears for later, preferring, I guess, to be alone with my grief.

Summer was pretty much over and I looked forward to school again, just so I could feel that things would get back to normal. I did make another trip to the woods, reliving the experience we had together. Daisy even seemed to sense that something was missing and only half-heartedly chased the squirrels.

I stopped playing solitaire basketball because it wasn't fun anymore without Aunt Edie being there to keep the score. I kept forgetting to keep track of who had the ball and who put it in the hoop. Someone once said that life is for the living.

It's terrible to admit, but that is absolutely the truth. As time went by I found that I didn't think about her every day any more. One morning I woke up for school and couldn't picture her face in my mind. I scrambled out of bed and quickly pulled her picture from my dresser drawer. My hands shook as I stared at her, feeling guilty and scared. How can we forget so quickly?

Within six months Uncle Eddie took early retirement and sold everything, the house and land included. He was so grief-stricken that he could not tolerate being near people or things which reminded him of Aunt Edie. Within one year he married a woman he met at a local meeting for people who have lost loved ones, and moved to Virginia. My mother and father visited him occasionally but he never came to Lima again.

I finally reached the point where I only thought of her at certain times, like holidays and her birthday. Two years after her death, Daisy had to be put to sleep. She was so full of arthritis that it was hard for her to get up the garage steps where she slept. My father took her to the veterinary after we all said our good-byes and she was mercifully put down. This was another link to Aunt Edie that was broken and I felt her loss all over again.

Most important of all are the things that Aunt Edie left us. Not money or objects to touch, but things like values, pride, and courage. I will never forget her dignity and grace. Ravaged by disease and sure in the knowledge that she would die, Aunt Edie never permitted her spirit to fade. Her life belonged to her, not to fear or bitterness, right to the very end. She also taught me to accept loss. She told me once that the next life is forever, and heaven must be huge to hold everyone who will go there. The earth is too small for all of us to be here forever.

I'll always remember her demand for perfection. Work wasn't to be done correctly, it was to be done perfect. She would rather have nothing be done at all than to tolerate poor craftsmanship. And she showed us love. I profited by having a "second mother," because I learned more about caring for others. Fortunately, I lived a childhood where I simply expected love from my mother and father because I always received it. Aunt Edie showed the value of love from someone outside the immediate home.

She will not be forgotten, thus she will live on even after I too am gone, because she taught me things that I have passed on to my son, and he will someday pass them along to his children. I can hear her yet today, sometimes when I walk through a stand of trees, or see a well-tended flower garden. A wheat field whispering in the wind can call out her name on the breeze, and these are the times when I smile at her memory and say to myself, "Thank you, Aunt Edie. I'll see you again some day soon."

978-0-595-00125-5
0-595-00125-4